THE DRUNKEN TOURIST

THE DRUNKEN TOURIST

CHRIS SANTANA

ISBN:978-0-9674056-2-9

Victor Press
1024 SW Main St. #644
Portland, OR 97205
VictorPress.org
VictorPressPub@gmail.com

Layout by Chris Krebs, *EvilEyeDesign@gmail.com*
Cover Photo by Josh Latham, www.joshlatham.us

This is a work of non-fiction. Some names and details have been altered to protect
the indentity of those involved, but the overall sequence of events is true to the best
of the author's memory.

Citations are included from:

> *Magister Ludi: The Glass Bead Game.* Herman Hesse. Bantam Books Edition.
> Introduction by Theodore Ziolowski.
> ISBN: 553 05555 150

> *The Urantia Book.* The URANTIA Foundation. Chicago: 1955

> *The Drunken Tourist.* Hadrian Santana. Victor Press.
> ISBN: 0-09674056-0-2

> *Alcoholics Anonymous. Third Edition.* Alcoholics Anonymous World Services, Inc.;
> New York City: 1976.**

**These excerpts from Alcoholics Anonymous are reprinted with the permission
of Alcoholics Anonymous World Service, Inc. ("A.A.W.S."). Permission to reprint
these excerpts does not mean that A.A.W.S. has reviewed or approved the contents
of this publication, or that A.A.W.S. necessarily agrees with the views expressed
herein. A.A. is a program of recovery from alcoholism only - use of these excerpts
in connection with programs and activities which are patterned after A.A., but which
address other problems, or in any other non-A.A. context, does not imply otherwise. Although Alcoholics Anonymous is a spiritual program, A.A. is not a religious
program, and use of A.A. material in the present connection does not imply A.A.'s
affiliation with or endorsement of, any sect, denomination, or specific religious belief.

To the Judge

A Sister of Christian Rehabilitation was soliciting funds at the bottom of the escalator. Our eyes met and I smiled first; therefore no donation necessary. Halfway up, I started digging for change, trying to figure the cost of my resentment towards the fact that her denomination had the best spot at the airport. "Hey Sister," I yelled down while warming up for a toss of the coin. She nodded that she was game, just as my own magical thinking bet the fate of the upcoming journey on our impending exchange. The sister let the coin come to her – a natural one-handed grab, shoulder high, almost casual. Right then and there I knew. My penchant for entertainment on the cheap would know no borders.

Los Angeles to Atlanta, Atlanta to Brussels, Brussels to Prague. Yeah buddy, I was off to the Czech Republic. Why? Because it was the farthest east I could go on my recently inherited 50,000 frequent flier miles on Delta. Included on the 50,000 was the return from Venice, with a jag in New York. Quite the deal compared to the 30,000 miles you have to subtract from your account for any domestic round trip, and these miles were expiring fast. Between a restraining order that had followed a lost custody battle, a probation department that had me by the balls, and the recently imposed banishment from my current Queen, what I needed to do was put some distance in between myself and this semblance of a life that seemed to be closing in on me so rapidly. Not to suggest that I was running away from my responsibilities or anything. After all, I had just put a check in the mail to Warner's lunch truck towards what I owed him for a month's worth of breakfast burritos.

Santana

I rolled to the gate and parked my suitcase next to the best looking female I could find without breaking stride. She was a beauty. Black canvas with the pop-up handle and good sized wheels. It was Bloomingdale's contribution to the trip, requisitioned during last week's shoplifting extravaganza. An item that begged to be taken out of the luggage department for a test drive through Housewares. The straps of the bag then had to be tested, slung over the same shoulder as my leather day bag which may have shielded the anti-theft sensor clip from the mother radar shields as I strolled straight out the door.

Thanks to Macy's there was no question that I looked the part of an important shopper. The shoe sale there had been a madhouse due to inconsiderate size 10½ shoppers leaving their unwanted pairs strewn around under the seats of the shoe department. There was also a gang of suits without the sensor clips which must have been returned recently. I found a Claiborne my size in a flat silver gray hanging out alongside its virgin brothers. The old khaki, washable Brooks Brothers I was wearing had to be sacrificed in the dressing room. I had another one anyway in an industrial blue that was actually holding up quite well through the wash. Both of them had been bought more than a year ago at the Hadassah Thrift on Lincoln and Santa Monica Boulevard for $9 each. It was the color of the Claiborne that sinned me.

After muddling through a surprisingly lax security check, I found seat 42A with the neighborhood conversation already in full swing. Natalie from San Diego had the aisle seat and was flirting away with two frat boys in the middle rows who were already sufficiently tanked. She was maybe twenty two, had just quit the job she hated, put her apartment up for sublet, left her cell phone at home and was spending the next two months on a backpacking tour through Europe. Of course she was a little nervous. A crossword puzzle was currently helping her hold steady. "Ladies and gentlemen, can I have your attention, please?" I hushed in a sarcastically authoritative tone, "could anyone help this young lady find a nine letter word for 'a strong desire?'" The cause was on. A wonderfully trivial cause. Our neighbors all introduced themselves with a few character defining mistakes. This I remember as part of the good spirit of travel – any excuse to get together and make the moment. We might eventually get 'hankering' but meanwhile the armrest between us was being shared liberally.

The Drunken Tourist

A distinctive change of atmosphere was in store for the Sabena connection from Atlanta to Brussels. Before I even sat down, I smelled something wasn't right. Stashing my big bag in the overhead compartment, I squinted around for the source of the stink. The couple directly behind my seat gazed at me in sober solidarity. They were both wearing hardened, veteran poses which I clearly read as, "Hey, it ain't us, and welcome to the suffering you are about to sit next to." Their eyes angled discreetly forward towards the seat next to mine. Sure enough, there was Ed, moving his briefcase to accommodate me, while the odor coming from his direction was wafting towards the center of the plane in a steady seepage. You figure an alarm would go off or something. This was no mere body odor. One look at him and you knew his cheeks were clenched, working hard at the imperative command of silent release. Any little peep from the seat and his cover would be thoroughly blown. Enter another spirit of travel, known as the old sympathy bond – instant camaraderie in the face of a common evil. 17C said it all with her lips drawn below her gums, exposing her bottom row of teeth, clenched in a, "Oh well, what can you do?" expression. You know - the one where your shoulders are all hunched up to meet your ears as your neck disappears in the cringe. I imitated back, adding a slight tilt of the head with a knowing nod.

Before losing consciousness, I decided to get up while there was still a chance to corner the stewardess at the serving station. Once there, I proceeded to relate the passing of the gas as delicately as possible, noting that I did have witnesses. A glazed, faraway look then caught hold of her, like she was being mystically transported by the promise of the smell. Intoxicatingly hypnotized, all she could do was come up with a well rehearsed, "I'm sorry sir, but as you can see, business class is completely full, there are no other seats available." "Well," I responded, "would you mind if I hung out by the lavatories for some fresh air before takeoff?" Nothing. She gave me no discernable reaction, not even a hint of recognition. It then crossed my mind that even as she continued to work at her station, she might still be romping through the fields of Odorland. Thank goodness she returned with the patented, "I'm sorry sir, please return to your seat. The fasten seatbelt sign has been turned on." As soon as her back was turned, I lifted two consolation Heinekens from the beverage cart and headed back to the ghetto.

Santana

After take-off, dinner was served, headsets were passed out and our movie started. Under the cover of relative darkness, coupled with the added diversion of audio, I guess Ed figured it was time to really let loose. In a matter of seconds the guy sitting in the seat directly in front of me stood up, turned around, and stared down at us, all teary-eyed. All I could do was look to 17C and pray she would support my innocence. No such luck. Her eyes were closed, her face taut, and another evacuation towards the bathrooms on my part could easily be misconstrued as an admission of collusion, if not outright conspiracy. Yet I looked up, an innocent man, calmly put my tray table into the upright position, put on my suit jacket, and proceeded to the front of the plane.

Near the forward cabin service station there was an open spot next to the emergency exit where crewmembers sit during take-off and landing. Within a minute, a steward popped out of the iron curtain of first class. He had a good swish going and a genuine smile.

"Good evening, sir," I ventured.

"And good evening to you, sir," he replied. "Nice suit, an excellent blue," he added as he got busy at the service station.

"Your suit's not bad for the standard issue," I responded in turn. "I believe you could have done a whole lot worse. Have you seen Delta's uniform this year?"

"My God," he whispered back, "did they merge with Burger King or what?" This guy was cool. "By the way, if you're waiting for the lavatory, I believe there is one open on the other side."

"No thanks," I replied, "just getting a little fresh air." I leaned closer to mention in confidence, one gentleman to another, "your partners in the back may have related to you the awkward situation in and around Row 17." I had his attention, explaining once again as delicately as possible the legend of the ill wind breaking mercilessly. The sympathy bond was back, this time with benefits. At Ed's unbeknownst expense, two men were bonding on a first class level. And that's just where he sent me, straight into first-class with my private little video monitor and a fresh Heineken. What luck! My man made it look like nothing more than an "appropriate" adjustment within standard protocol.

I credit the suit. Italian silk in a durable dark blue, bought at the thrift store for $18, then tailored for another $22. I always dress well

The Drunken Tourist

for any flight and had made a conscious decision to pack only my best for this trip. I went with two suits, the grey and the blue, one pair of black trousers that worked well with the jackets, a fine light brown suede waistcoat, and of course, my black trenchcoat. Two out of the three pants had two back pockets with buttons to secure, while the blue suit's pants and the slacks had that rare mini pocket on the inside right. When I bought the brown suede, I haggled the price down due to a rip in the outside handkerchief pocket. I had planned to sew it up, but realized the rip made for an additional stash, hard to detect. A money belt for traveling had been recommended by just about everybody, but after a test walk I found that it inhibited my stride and once I needed something from it the secret was out anyway. I ended up using it only when I slept.

As a rule, my left back pocket would house: 1) my return plane ticket (if lost, I would have to pay whatever fare was available, then hassle for my refund in 90 days – it was as if Delta was banking that I would lose it): 2) my Eurail pass good for five days of traveling within a two month time frame: and 3) an old AmTrak voucher, good for a one way trip anywhere in the States. All three of them were then tucked inside the pages of my passport and rubber banded together. The right back pocket had my wallet with an emergency $50, pictures of Paramahansa Yogananda, my son Alexander, and my favorite likeness of Christ. An expired California driver's license and a debit card from a recently closed account were included for the taking, if need be.

The key bundle had my versateller card and my drivers license, along with a folded photocopy of my passport. This was either going into the handkerchief pocket stash or the front left pocket. The right front always had my spending cash. No keys, no phone.

I tried the inside of my shoes for a stash, but feared the versateller card would crack on the run and it might look suspicious through security. As it turned out, I usually felt secure enough to put the real cards with the tickets, all bundled together with the passport. The wallet with the dummies was always available as the most obvious sacrifice for thieves if there had to be one.

Packing only one good white dress shirt and one tie proved to be a mistake. Dressing up really does wonders for a broke hangover. Instead I relied on two short sleeve polo shirts, one black and one blue that looked good with the suits either tucked in or not. Three V-necked undershirts, a guinea T, six pairs of new socks and boxers finished off the big bag, weighing in at maybe fifty pounds. My shoulder bag was old classic brown leather, customized with snap buckles. That garage sale bag got more attention than anything else. It was a great conversation piece while cosigning the misconception that I was a seasoned traveler or something. The Urantia Book took up almost a third of the bag along with Herman Hesse's "Magister Ludi," which was pretty thick, too. My notebook was slim enough, leaving room for a little Big Book of AA and Yogananda's "Metaphysical Meditations." A sheet music book with a hundred or so standards would have been worth its weight in gold, but I didn't figure it. Stocking up on vitamins would have been another good bet. Shampoo and such seemed way too bulky to consider, so I didn't. A plastic soap dish would prove to be the one item I missed the most and couldn't find when I remembered to shop for it. Yeah, I thought I had it going on all right. Everything nice and tight, except for the fact that my face was a mess and gave it all away. At this point the airlines were more apt to check in the baggage under my eyes than the stolen luggage. My inside jacket pockets held both my day shades and my "glasses" that were bogus dummies, lightly tinted, designed for indoor and night time vanity purposes. I guess some people can hide a few months of serious drinking, heartbreak, and crack smoking better than others. Still, I figured I could get by – I would just avoid all overhead fluorescent lighting like an ageing primadonna that couldn't afford a facelift.

* * *

There was a three hour layover in Brussels before the one hour flight to Prague. The terminal bar featured sixteen ounces of excellent local beer on tap for about four bucks. The bartender was not concerned about how many I already had, I didn't have to change money and he didn't ask me to show I.D. This was my first clue to a major shift in policy between continents. And this was just at the airport. Soon to be discovered was the only reliable international exchange rate indicator I would come to rely on - the most common denominator of the civilized world: the price of a good beer.

The Drunken Tourist

I met Soren at the gate for Prague. He had that look about him that said, "Hey, I can help if you need anything." I acknowledged him but did not press.

I sat within comfortable earshot and took out Hesse to get centered. My new hero was the Magister Ludi, just starting to hear his call towards self-realization. I admired his voice of reason from the very first chapter. A few pages well read could lead me to adopt his tone.

"Do you speak any English?" I asked for the first time in a long time.

"I certainly do," he replied with a German accent.

"You are off to Prague, then?" I asked in this phrasing that I would never use at home.

"To Praha, yes." The education had started. "Is this your first time there?"

"Yes, yes, my first time," I responded with that curious phrasing again. "And for you?"

"Well, I am there quite often on business, but this weekend I am going for a short holiday," he said with a wide smile.

"Well then, congratulations," I said. "We are both on holiday – how about a beer?"

"Of course," he answered in a heartbeat, "but only if you let me buy."

"If you insist, of course," I replied, of course.

Soren was working for Prince Cigarettes in the marketing department. He was a bit tore up about utilizing his talents to promote a cause that was questionable at best. He also really enjoyed the money. And, with a little creative scheduling, the perks included weekend jaunts to places like Praha. He proceeded to enthusiastically map out the town and recommended that I stay at Jana Holukanova's boarding house in Prague 4. A bit of a walk from the center he noted, but well worth it.

Upon our arrival at the airport in Prague, he escorted me to the exchange window. I willingly gave him a $100 that he included with his Deutschmarks. He could have ripped me off right there, but instead we split a cab to Jana's. Taxis in this town, he explained, were notorious for overcharging.

By the time we pulled up in front of the three story townhouse it must have been well past midnight. I can't say I remember. It would be sufficient to say I was thoroughly inebriated at this point. As he introduced me at the door, he must have explained to Jana that he had reservations elsewhere. It was easy to tell by the tone of the conversation that my host was voicing her concerns in regards to the obvious wreckage she was looking to check in. Soren reassured her I was to be trusted and would pay a week's stay in advance. Jana then led me to a clean room on the second floor. The double bed had a Van Gogh above it and the windows opened out to the back yard with a box of geraniums in full bloom on the sill. I felt like quite the Steppenwolf peeling off my long black trench as I settled in. The deal was struck at $90 US for the week, including laundry and breakfast, ready any time before noon. Soren would see us tomorrow.

BAD HOOD TO GET LOST IN
SLUM BEER
JUNKIE PARK
SLUM SPEED
HOSTEL
METRO STATION
FINE ARTS
JUST RIGHT
NARODNI
ROCK & PUNK CLUBS
HOOKERS
MUSIC STORES
TOO CROWDED
JAMMIN
DISCO CASINO
CHELSEA'S JAZZ
GREAT SAUSAGE
SUNSET GARDENS
JAZZ & BLUES CLUB
KATERINA'S PUPPY HOUSE
DANCE CLUBS
VIEWS A'PLENTY
QUIET
SWEET PARK
JO'S BAR
UP the Hill
JANA'S PLACE
NAT. MUSEUM
GOLDEN
John Lennon's WALL
St. Nicks
LANE
Opera
STROLLING
CHARLES BRIDGE
TWILIGHT TIME
ALONG
Killer clock
NICE
CENTER Pile o' LEAD
BEATLES PONTOON BAR
KAFKA'S BAR
Jewish Quarter
GOOD AREA TO GET LOST IN
TRAIN STATION
MISHKA'S SUNGLASS HUT

Prague

Hey, I just woke up in the middle of Europe. What had taken me so long? And who had made every window frame I passed a thing of beauty, every giant stone and tiny tile an integrated part of this work of art they're calling Praha? Who needed a map? I was happily lost and completely disoriented in this freakin' fairy tale of a town. Walking down the hill from Jana's house, arms swinging wide, completely unprepared for the history surrounding me, I blew by the National Museum and a few impressive churches without regret. It was all right here in front of me. I might have time for them later.

The first real discovery of the day was my newly established 1.5 Second Road Rule: if eye contact is made in passing, and that contact is held for 1.5 seconds, an acknowledgement of some kind is absolutely required. Oh dear, I thought, the unspoken shame if there was no reciprocation. Stuck with the luggage of regret as you shuffle off with all that missed opportunity to carry. "The disappointments hardest to bear are those which never come!"

No one would find me in violation of the 1.5 Second Rule today. In fact, I seemed to be such a curious looking fellow that adherence to it was practically guaranteed. It must be the walk – I hadn't felt this free in years. Plus, I had a new tune working:

> *You can nod or something, say anything,*
> *Who cares who's listening, it's probably just the usual*
> *But if you keep on walking and say your little prayers*
> *And you believe in spirit beings, they might be listening too.*

Santana

A beer was certainly in order. And with it, I was able to implement my benchmark indicator theory established the day before at Brussels airport. The beer was cold and strong. It was just dry enough and cost me the equivalent of about a buck fifty, served by a smiling local beauty at a table in the sun. Therefore, I could safely assume that Prague was an excellent vacation value. Of course I would have to do a great deal more research before I could put this measure up for canon law. Could this theory become a rule after 1,327 beers in 114 different neighborhoods in 23 cities within 14 countries? We would have to suffer through and see. Meanwhile, the more pressing question was whether this young lady could make her stare my way any more obvious while her man was sitting with his back to me.

I hate that shit no matter where I go. That extra long look that smells like a broken commandment. Green light power in the hands of pretty girls is such a threat. Don't these ladies know that when they work that look they are involuntarily enlisting in the camp of my archenemies? After all, I need to be the one in charge – praising the Lord with a benevolent hard-on while battling this outrageously appropriate type of yuppie as they prance around flexing their own overblown sense of entitlement. This all called for another brew. Yet what I could really use was a piano.

Back in May, I had broke down and learned a couple of standards, while the tunes that I had written with vocals could now be taken care of with the melody lines reworked for the right hand on the piano. These recycled songs, along with three new instrumental numbers comprised a sparkling set of about twenty three minutes. Another half an hour or so could be improvised with those tired, melancholy chord changes I had been settling on for years. This way, I figured I might be able to get a couple of happy hour gigs on the road for a day or two, then move on before my limited repertoire would inevitably be exposed. Today I was feeling so on top of my game that I did not doubt the value of my services for a minute. I pressed on in confidence, clueless to this obvious connection to my failed relationships and lack of perseverance.

I found the Sunset Garden by default. It was across the street from the Jazz and Blues Club, Praha's largest venue for jazz. When I made bold to ask the Blues Club's boss for a gig on the spot,

The Drunken Tourist

he practically laughed me out the door. The guy must have been trained in New York. The Sunset Garden, however, was desperate enough to consider hiring me. With neither sunset nor garden in sight, it was the only bar I had been to all day that wasn't packed. Inconveniently located a good fifty yards off the street, there was only a little wooden triangle sign standing on the main sidewalk to advertise its benefits. The owners were natives in their mid-forties, dressed in a mid-eighties East Village leather style, complete with the Beatle Boots, toned down mullets, and those belt clips for cell phones. Once our mutual cool guard was vanquished with the help of Mr. Pilsner Urquel, I was more than happy to play my part between four and six for dinner and drinks.

I figured it this way; the staff and their eight or ten loyal patrons would be sick of my shtick in a couple of days, so why not play it up as the hunched over, unpredictable, offbeat piano player who drank too much? I could work the pose of a semi-tragic stranger who might be casually exhibiting accidental flashes of brilliance that were actually my most tired licks interjected just in time to save a new progression that I was too afraid to resolve right there and then. This way, I had all my bases covered: 1) I didn't have to be that good, 2) the pity party was on, 3) no, I didn't take requests, and 4) yes, I would take another hit and have another cocktail. The drug of choice was hashish cigarettes, rolled with such tenderness, quietly and casually passed around.

Prague was a different town once twilight set in. Gone were half the uncoordinated tourists lugging around their vacation faces, dressed in flaming ensembles they would never try at home. Enter pure gold. The spotlights on the buildings and statues now worked an art form all their own. I ended up alone and lost again as I followed the footpath running parallel with the Vltava River. I had a nice buzz going anyway, and really, how lost could I be? Feeling sufficiently satisfied with the progress of the day, I could easily dispel this ideal opportunity for a little soul searching and just take it all in.

By the time I found my way to the Charles Bridge it must have been past ten. The ancient statues of the Saints that had long ago been eternally secured on the railing were now surrounded by parties of tourists and locals alike.

Santana

The few who were drinking and smoking were going about it with nonchalance and discretion. I noticed only one pair of policemen across the whole expanse and they were primarily concerned with everyone staying off the statues. There was a very practical, mutual respect going on here. Something unheard of where I come from.

A guitar player started what soon became a Nirvana sing along. By the time the second chorus came around, almost everyone was wailing, "No, I don't have a gun, no I don't have a gun." What an anthem. It was perfect. I felt the air of excellent timing. No singular cause was dominating the moment. International feel was the order of the day. Universal appeal couldn't help but follow. Economically good times must also be credited.

Take our little group from Poland, for instance. Goshka and her brother and his two buddies were on holiday from the university. Goshka was able to express herself a bit bolder now that she was out of her hometown for the weekend. She could reach out to a guy like me while feeling protected enough by her entourage, primarily because they could all finally afford to take a little trip together. Destination Prague had been somewhat determined by her love of Franz Kafka. The means to get here had been somewhat determined by the raise her dad got working for a fish company that had a good year due to some hatchery in the Black Sea that the new guard of the old Soviet Politburo had to farm out for cash during one of those ruble emergencies most likely due to Lord knows what level of old guard mismanagement and greed.

Today, we could safely assume the spirit of the Velvet Revolution was still alive and well. I was always a little bit jealous of not being around during those types of dramatic events – growing up idolizing characters a few years older who had done their part in those times which had historically given them a defining credibility.

So what were we doing about it tonight? Well, even while some of us still needed an intoxicant to get us to what was really on the menu, the honest ones knew it certainly wasn't about the drink and drug. It was something stronger – you could taste it. The truth of the moment was the power; the energy shared, consciously and creatively multiplied. As I rode this power to the capital Kingdom of the Present, a holy spirit harnessed my undivided attention and my mind

The Drunken Tourist

dropped into the bubbling, bottomless well of my heart. The pulse of current life was now enough – completely whole, paramount and meaningful in and of itself.

I saw the tanks of today as personal. The absence of a big bad wolf occupying the territory could only help take us further. We could stretch together while holding our own. We could also choose to humble down a little and try another stretch if the current stretch sucked. Sort of like Disco. Historians could decide later what was historic.

* * *

I took it slower the following day, deliberately. After firing up the hot water heater for a bath, I brushed my teeth methodically for a long time. I dispensed with my usual frantic blur of the brush stroke that sometimes left my gums bleeding while getting into the differences in the plumbing and the toiletries and the doorknobs, etc. It was all so new and so quaint and so fascinating for about ten minutes. Jana was making just enough noise to let me know she was in the kitchen mothering the breakfast spread. A variety of pork products would be waiting.

After crossing the Charles Bridge again, I caught sight of a stick figure walking about a block ahead of me. I doubled my pace, passed her, then circled back around through the crowd, making sure our eyes met just as I looked away. Around the next corner it turned out we were walking right next to each other. How about that.

"Excuse me," I asked, "was that you a few blocks down?" I smiled and made a full circle with my arm and pointed back.

"Oh yes, the block down?" as she motioned and kept walking.

"You speak English then, yes?" I carried on.

She squinted her eyes and held her thumb a small space between her forefinger. "A little. What it is you need?" she said slowly. I felt like an idiot teenager and looked around for anyone who might be an American who could plainly see through this thin line of bullshit.

"I don't need anything. I am very happy today." She didn't get it, but I had her attention. So I did the old me and you hand gesture, followed by the drink gesture, then the wristwatch gesture.

"Do you have time for a drink," came out more than a little lame.

Santana

"Yes, I do, but you – how do you say – you exaggerate?"
She was very cute.

"Yes, yes, I do," again with that curious phrasing, "I like very
much to exaggerate – like I said, I am very happy today. I feel like
(pausing to exaggerate) goofing around."

"What is this goofing?"

"Like horseplay."

"You are playing now?"

"No, no. Just goofing around, you know."

"You are silly then." It was useless, but who cared. I wanted horseplay.

We walked well together. From what I gathered, Katerina was out
getting lost in town, too. She might have recently moved here from a
little town about two hours south of the city. I wasn't certain. Either
that or she was going to move there in an hour or two. We definitely
did share a few good "oohs" and "aahs" brought on by a statue of
some god holding up the moon and a fountain that offered some
relief from the heat. It seemed like this might be a good time to invest
in an English/Czech pocket dictionary. It was less than a buck and
Katerina was very impressed. We were now off to any bar in earnest,
giddy with the thought of further communication.

Lemonade and vodka was served with pen and paper. She looked
up and wrote down 'hospital' then wrote 'friends' then '8:00'.

"You are meeting friends from the hospital at eight?" I tried.

"Yes, yes," she was so pleased.

I followed by finding the Czech word for 'work,' then pointing
back to "hospital" then saying "you?" as I pointed to her. I finished
with, "You work at hospital?"

She laughed, "No no no," and grabbed the book.

"I… have… (oh no) …sickness… (the suspense was real now) …
head. She stuck with, "I have sickness head." Well there ya' have
it. She looked up at me and shrugged it off with a kooky grin while
knocking on her skull a few times.

I believe this gesture was to assure me that her condition was
either nothing to take seriously or there was nothing she could do
about it. She was so casual about the whole thing that I figured it had
to be a plus anyway you looked at it.

She was beaming all right. But now I couldn't tell whether she was smiling because she was proud of herself for looking up the sentence or proud of her condition. I asked for the blasted book back and did the old catch up to me in the drink department gesture while I took my turn looking something up. When I got back to her she was still working on that kooky smile of hers. Now I couldn't tell if she was smiling because she was having a good time, or just being polite, or what. I wrote down in Czech, "my friends," then pointed to her 'sickness head.' Oh, how we laughed… and oh, how I wanted to burn that little rat bastard book page by page.

Instead, she continued our incredibly irritating exercise with, "I…have…(here we go)….puppy…(what?) …house."

"You have puppy house?" Of course she did. We smiled and nodded. After all, doesn't everybody have puppy house around here? "I have a puppy at my house," was the verdict.

This conversation was actually degenerating rapidly. Still, I persevered without the fucking book, "I love puppies. Can I come and see?" Oh, how we laughed…and oh, how I certainly would down another cocktail.

Before she had to go we strolled on towards the Sunset Garden and agreed to meet tomorrow at 4:00. We really did walk well together. Eventually, she was the one that ended up suggesting very casually that we go to my place and go to bed. I was the one that ended up feeling guilty as her emerald eyes rolled all the way back towards the top of that suspect skull of hers while I moved inside her. Her skin was perfectly taut and she shivered a little, too. She was sure enjoying herself. She and Jana even got along. They met when she left my room to use the bathroom. In fact, everyone was comfortable with our little situation except me. I suppose I was not as disenfranchised from Americana as I had thought.

That American thought proved contagious – I went ahead and planned the next day. I figured while I was at it, I might as well take in some of the official culture. Halfway down the hill I fell in earshot of an English couple:

"Do you want to eat first, or get the tickets for the outdoor opera tonight and then eat?"

"How close are we?" he replied. "Isn't the ticket booth right next to St. Nicholas?"

"Why don't we stop and check the map."

"If we stop we might as well eat."

"But if we eat we might miss out on the tickets again."

"I don't want to rush like yesterday. I thought we were going to the Norodni Museum this afternoon anyway."

"Whatever's good for you, dear."

"Come on now, honey," he replied. "I don't want to do everything I want to do. Where do you want to go?"

"I thought the Norodni then the opera was a good plan, dear, but first I would like to eat."

"O.K. sweetheart. Where do you want to eat?"

"I don't care, let's try a different route and maybe we'll get lucky."

"O.K. then," he said. "We can either check the map while we're walking and see where we are or we can just continue down the hill and then go whichever way looks good."

"O.K. then. But you get to choose the restaurant."

Man, was I glad to be traveling alone. And these guys were being really nice to each other. Then again, it was still early. Then again, what did I know about traveling as a couple?

The Church of St. Nicholas had an admission charge of what might have amounted to fifty cents. Yet it was just enough for me to conjure up the biblical Jesus driving the merchants from the temple. Why should I pay admission into my Father's house? The woman at the collection booth tried to stop me twice. At first I played dumb and then I turned around and shushed her and kept moving. I went on through, but my indignant attitude that had been so swiftly adopted in the name of half a buck would prevent me from enjoying the experience. Instead I felt the need to defend my ridiculous position by privately contending that the whole layout of the church was way too busy. Every little spot in it had some intricacy that had been detailed during the evil pastime of trying to materialize the spiritual. I walked out in a huff and found Jo's Bar right across the street. Roxy Music was on and I quickly spent ten times the entrance fee of St. Nick's on two beers. What a talent I had for losing it so rapidly. Thirty minutes ago I was thinking that I was some sort of invincible supernatural lightning rod. Once again, I realized that what I was thinking really didn't count for much. What I did was the true story. I went back

The Drunken Tourist

to apologize to the woman and put the donation where it belonged. I figured as far as these ancient houses of God were concerned, I would either pay or not go in. All other attractions however, were still fair game.

Jo's Bar turned out to be one of the best in town. The blokes from Great Britain didn't threaten me; it was the Americans I was looking to avoid. Mahalo Glen's Jazz Club down the street housed the cocky fellows from L.A. and New York. Every other nationality I ran into happily hung out together, while we Americans just seemed to threaten each other overseas. Again, that overblown sense of entitlement was rearing its ugly head, this time in the name of control.

The owner turned out to be a typical American ex-pat lightweight who probably couldn't make it as a waiter in New York but had found the dollars back in the early 90s to open a bar. Now he played the big shot as a club owner in Prague. You bet I was jealous. The good news was the cook was selling hash for about $10 US a gram. I picked one up along with a Herald Tribune. There was also the Prague Post in English, so I checked the classifieds thoroughly. It looked like a small apartment in a good neighborhood could be found through the paper for about $400 US. From my experience this meant with a little footwork you could probably score a really nice place for about the same, probably less. The service work wages, however, were terribly low. This town seemed like an ideal place to set up shop, not work in one.

I continued along the river, passing John Lennon's Wall and the park ending at the Noradni Bridge. There was a handful of homeless folk on the way, sharing space with the kids out for the weekend. Neither left any evidence of disrespect. The train station across the bridge was where the junkies were and the neighborhood in back of that was a little ghetto. Speed was the deal of the day – powder that burned. It would likely take a good half an hour to kick in so I grabbed a nasty beer at some pit that reminded me of the Circle Bar on 7th and B in the East Village. After one swill I figured it was a good idea to move. Everybody there looked broke. Once out the door, I didn't even have to look back to know I was being followed. Turning a quick corner, I raced back toward the train station. Still running a block and a half later, I saw a sign that read "Hostel $12 US".

Santana

The door was not open and the buzzer didn't ring. I looked both directions down the street, then took a few steps back and looked up to the second floor, shouted hello, then knocked on the window. There was no one in sight, but still I was sweating it. The rush of the run must have kicked in the speed. A fellow finally came down to answer the door and point out the sign that read "Full".

I asked him for a minute and he let me in. After giving him the prospective client bullshit so he would let me use the bathroom, I sucked up the rest of the speed and tried to chill out for a minute. Yeah right. I was spun.

Once out of the neighborhood, my sense of well-being returned with a vengeance. How much of it was the speed and how much of it was me motivated in the current of the day was a tired question, best left for after I came down from whatever it was that was presently working.

As I waited for Goshka to meet me at the bridge, I found myself admiring a few handsome couples strolling by, wondering how many really good looking people are seriously handicapped in character development due to the gravity of the mirror. Goshka didn't have to worry about any of that. She not only knew it, she used it to her advantage. The only must-see of the day for her was the Kafka Museum, the only must-see for me were those two beautiful breasts currently saluting half the town. I promptly admitted it to her and she took it as a compliment and laughed me off. Her focus remained firm. Yet another quality to admire as we headed to the Jewish Quarter by way of Starometske Square. We loved the clock, had trouble with the statue in the center of the square, and then did a very quick perusal of the Bethlehem Church.

I was on the lookout for a non-suffering depiction of the Christ for a change. By the time I had exhausted this theme for the day, I counted 14 Christs nailed to the cross compared to two of the living, breathing Jesus. One was Him as an infant, the other was from the free postcard rack at the Kafka Café. This likeness featured His flaming heart exposed but still with the crown of thorns. The resurrected Christ had his left hand opening the robe while the right hand had that pointed pose, inviting us to share the goods. Both wounds were still healing. So technically this Christ did qualify as living and

The Drunken Tourist

breathing. He certainly was living, while the breathing situation had probably been solved a few days ago.

I remember how Goshka noticed the transformation to reverence in people's faces when they viewed a work of art. We communicated well enough to discuss the brilliance of the artwork that commanded the viewer's attention versus that same viewer's predisposition towards self-forgetting. One thing was for sure, our conversations put us in a different ballpark than Katerina's puppy house.

We spent the rest of the evening with Goshka's brother. He was still juiced from the energy share of the night before. Jo's Bar finished us off. Three sweaty floors packed with European youngsters on holiday revealing the season's new style of underwear. The music was a good mix of rock&roll and hip hop with a number of trance music songs that could have been the same trance music song. I can't remember. It was like a trance or something.

* * *

Breakfast was still there at noon, with a note from Jana. I read it as "Katerina will meet you at Shoske Station at four o'clock. Take the #3 to Praha 5." A trolley ticket and a map were enclosed with the note.

Completely hungover, I downed a breakfast beer and headed for the train stop. By the time I figured out how to use my ticket, I noticed it was practically optional.

The route hugged half the circumference of Praha 1, the old town I had been working by foot. It was nice to be cruised around the city for a change. I made it by 3:30. There was a fountain sculpture that I parked next to and tried to get into a little Hesse, but between the heat and the night before, I felt I would pass out before the end of the chapter.

I bought a nectarine from the fruit stand and approached this teenager selling sunglasses. "Do you speak any English?" I asked for the hundredth time this week.

"Yes, a little," she replied.

"Well, I was hoping you could do me a favor," I said, as I took my sunglasses off and smiled a tired smile. "I am supposed to meet someone here at four o'clock. Did you see a very thin young lady with curly, black hair and green eyes?"

Santana

"No, I don't think so" she said. "She sounds hard to miss."

"Yes, she is. This is Shotske Station in Praha 4, isn't it?" I asked, already knowing.

She sighed, "Yes it is. I am here every day."

"You speak excellent English. Thank you for your help."

She answered proudly, "I go to English school three nights a week."

"Hey, that's great. Could you do me a favor? Keep an eye out for her, I'll be over there by the fountain. I fear I'm going to have to pass out for a while."

"Of course," she laughed. "Business is very slow. I will be here only one hour more."

"That's perfect," I replied. "Thank you very much."

Sure enough, Mishka, the teenage sunglass salesgirl, roused me in an hour. I woke up all groggy, "No sign of her, eh?"

"I'm sorry, sir," she said sincerely.

"Do you know the expression, 'stood up?'" I asked.

"Yes, yes," she replied. "This happens to everybody."

They sure grow up fast around here. "I could use a cup of coffee. Would you like to join me, yes?" again with the lingo.

"I would like to join you, but I have to pack up. If you could wait, I would like Tequila." What? Did I just hear Tequila? Tequila means sexual possibilities where I come from. A second ago I wasn't even entertaining the idea this fresh face was even remotely interested in my hungover ass.

Mishka was very straightforward. "Do you know that I have to sell four pairs of sunglasses in a day just to get paid? Today I sold one. My boyfriend's family got me the job. Now I have to see him every day. I'm just not that crazy about him, you know?" I knew it. Here we go with the boyfriend blues. What was I thinking, anyway? Now I would have to abide by my own rules about this stuff.

"Do you tell him you drink with hungover foreigners?" I asked.

"He accuses me of everything and then he says he doesn't care about any of it," she replied.

"Well, is he ever right?" I asked. Her look back at me said it all and put some weight in my drawers.

"Why don't we eat," I declared once we sat down. I figured, why not? The place was a little pricey on the Tequila but the food was cheap.

The Drunken Tourist

Plus, I had a better chance of holding steady on a full stomach. The girl was naughty-gorgeous.

There was a birthday party going on at a long table in the same room. We got into the sing along with them and when somebody broke out a Polaroid camera I volunteered to take a couple of photos for them. Turns out the Czechs really dig their old school too, and even I could handle a Polaroid. Everyone was in such suspense while the pictures developed. Then they insisted that we pull our chairs close together for a shot of us next. Mishka and I were suddenly arm and arm. We stayed that way after the shot was taken. A squeeze on the shoulder and a rub on each other's back naturally followed.

Mishka reached down for the inside of my leg and started rubbing my cock on the outside of my pants. I had room to grow with her touch. Our kisses were soft with our mouths very open. She liked to press a little on my bottom lip. She soon took my hand in hers and guided me towards her belly and the bottom of her breasts, just barely brushing her nipples. Now she needed something more in her mouth. She looked at me while she sucked on my forefinger, her other hand still rubbing the length of my erection. I leaned over and whispered, "I want inside you." She nodded, still sucking, still looking straight at me. Nobody noticed or nobody cared.

"How much time do you have?" I asked.

"I don't know," she answered as she looked around.

"I meant what time do you have to be home."

"Oh, I have to be back at 7:30 to call my mother."

"Back where?"

"Back at my boss' house."

"How long on the train from here?"

"Only one half an hour."

"And how long is it to your boss' house from Charles Bridge?"

"Not far at all, I can walk there in ten minutes time."

"Well good. Do you like smoking hash?"

"Oh, yes."

"O.K. then, we can do that before you go if you like."

"Of course I like."

Reefer or hash discouraged me sexually but surely I would not be in any danger of that here. What I really was afraid of was that one of us might have a little morality attack and we might need another reason to go back to my place. Then again, I really didn't think there was any real danger of that happening either. I was just looking out for that fine line between flirtation and penetration that might be easier to live with later.

"Mishka, could you order two more drinks while I use the phone, please?"

"Of course, of course," she said, of course.

I calculated that it was morning in Los Angeles. The day before yesterday I had finally figured out the pre-paid phone card deal. I called my old mate Ron at Unified Photo.

"Unified Photo, this is Cindy, how can I help you?"

"Cindy, this is Chris, how the hell are you?"

"How am I? Where the fuck are you?"

"I'm in Prague."

"You're in where?"

"I'm in Prague, you know, Central Europe. I had to take some time off… I sort of squared it with Daryl before I left. He thinks I'm in jail."

"What did you tell him, that old restraining order story of yours?"

"Yes, as a matter of fact. Didn't Ron say anything to anybody?"

"You mean the same Ron that's been covering for you for the last six months, that Ron?"

"Yeah, that Ron. Is he around?"

"He's here tough guy; can you hold on a second?"

"You bet. Thanks, Cindy."

"Take care of yourself, you knucklehead. Hold on, he's right here."

"O.K. thanks," The phone picked right back up.

"This is Ron. How can I help you?"

"Ron, it's me. I'm in Prague."

"You fucker, you went through with it. Everybody here thinks you're in jail."

"Sorry to disappoint you pal, but what I need today is to place an order. I have to hurry, I don't know how much time I have left on this phone card."

"Can't you call me back on the 800 number?"

"I tried that, it's only good in the continental United States."

The Drunken Tourist

"Never mind why on earth you want to order anything, just tell me how are you going to pay for it."

"Well, technically I'm still an employee, right?"

"Oh come on. Don't fuck with me."

"O.K. you're right, let's open a new account under my name and give me 30 days to pay. I'll secure the order on my debit card so we're safe, O.K.?"

"O.K., that might work, but as you know, 'the shipping might kill you.'"

"How could I forget? What's the price and availability on the grey market Polaroid?"

"Well, we still have a ton of it with an August expiration date. Bruce can't even get rid of it. I can let you have it at cost."

"Beautiful, but the shipping might kill me. Could you find out the UPS charges and start with an order for ten of the ten shot boxes? I'll have Gordon drop off my camera tomorrow and I'll call you back in a couple of hours." I was sure we would be cut off in a second. "You know I just opened a whole new territory for you, tough guy."

"I can't believe you. Give me the address."

"I'll call with that later, our time is running out, just get the estimate for Prague in the Czech Republic."

"I know where Prague is, big shot. Did I mention the shipping might kill you?"

"Will you shut the fuck up already? How's Harry?"

"He's right here, sitting at your desk. He told me to tell you the shipping might kill you." (This was our manager's favorite sales tool that he never let us forget. He'd just figure the cost of shipping into the price of the film to make the customer feel they were getting a better deal. At least we got a lot of mileage out of this lame close.)

"Well, God bless ya," I said, almost sarcastically, "I'll talk to you later; the postcard's in the mail." It was good to speak a little American for a change.

I headed back to the table to check the feasibility of my plan with my new assistant. Mishka was getting sick. I suggested a cab back to my place so she could lie down for a while. Half of the restaurant tab was regurgitated in two equal increments during the ride there.

Out of the cab, into my room and onto the bed, Mishka revived in no time. What a relief. The moment, however, was certainly over. We split a beer, talked about taking the photos, and played around a bit, but that was about it. For what it was worth, I suppose it worked for both of us.

A recovery day was long overdue, as witnessed from my toes to my hair when I came to. Back in New York it had become tradition to try to spend this time all day at the movies. It kept my thinking off me. If I had any money left from the last binge, I would dress up as best I could, buy a bottle of wine and boost a sandwich or two before I dragged my sorry ass to what had become a steady rotation of any given Cineplex that fit the bill. If I could stand the wait, I would hang out by the exit door for the end of the last show, acting all exasperated, asking anyone for their ticket stub.

If somebody came out and lit up a smoke, I would approach them first, explaining that I had just come out to smoke before my movie started and couldn't find my stub. That fellow smoker usually bought it, didn't buy it and didn't care, or else was happy enough that I didn't try to bum a smoke to start digging for their old ticket. Otherwise something like, "please, I've got to get back in, I think I lost my keys," might work, too. If all else failed, I would just walk in and explain the same to the attendee while slowing down but not completely breaking stride. After all, I was stressed, and those were my keys, and I wanted to get back in there before the next show started. From there it was easy not to think about the debacle of the previous run. And depending on what was playing, chances were good I could get all misty during the corny parts. The more wrecked I was, the easier it was to get a few good tears out. Some days I was in such bad shape that I would well-up during the previews. On more than one occasion I stayed until the end of the last show, found a vacant theater that had already been cleaned, laid out under the stage behind the curtain and crashed. When I heard the vacuum cleaner going around ten the next morning, I brushed myself off and hit the streets. This was risky and done only in extreme circumstances. It was always better for everyone if I hung around until the last show was about to start. Right about then as I checked my pockets, I would ask for a stub from someone settled in their seats, explaining that I wanted to go out for a smoke before our feature was about to begin. Stub in hand, I'd

The Drunken Tourist

explain to the employee at the ticket booth that I had just received an emergency call and had to go. It was a real shame; I couldn't see the show that I was really looking forward to, asked if they had seen it, was it any good, and could I please have my money back? Nine times out of ten I got away with it. If my unsuspected sponsor had paid for the show by credit card, they gave me a free pass to come back next time. If I was lucky and they paid with cash, I walked out with a profit. Technically, this was all out thievery, and technically I had few qualms about ripping off Hollywood and company. They had been ripping me off for years.

At about three bucks a show and a bar in every other movie house in Prague, these types of moves were not so necessary. At Lucerna, the Czech equivalent of an old fashioned mall, located at the bottom of Wenceslaus Square, there were two theaters to choose from, both built in the early nineteen hundreds. Lucerna Cinema Café was a beautiful bar on its own, preserved in original art deco style with a grand piano and a great view of the throngs walking through the enclosed passages below. The regulars were a mix of older locals all dressed in their everyday best, a sizable Arab contingent and the modest Africans, a few Italians and French, along with the young American and British ex-pats being the loudest of the crowd.

I shared a beer with Patrick Cunnigham, a writer from San Diego in his sixties, living quite comfortably on his Social Security from the States and engaged to be married to a Czech woman considerably younger than he was.

Michal and Jitka were working the bar with their sincere Czech hospitality smiles and a standard "Dobre den" (good day) or "Ciao," which everyone says for either hello or goodbye. These guys were typical Czech youngsters – independent, modest yet self-assured, bilingual, and dedicated to accommodating my hangover. Michal gave me the lay of the land. Everyone here pretty much got along just fine. The Africans, the Arabs, the Americans and the Europeans all felt so grateful to live here instead of their own native land that it eclipsed all inherent differences coming from home. On the other hand, the Czechs were used to playing host, whether they wanted to or not. Their tiny republic had been trampled on and occupied for so many centuries by so many different aggressors, it must have

Santana

been ingrained in their social metabolism to accept, adjust, and make the best of it. This was something uniquely Czech, and they were as proud of it as they were as proud of their beer and their women. Meanwhile, if I had bought the whole bar a round, it might have worked out to maybe twenty bucks, considering half the crowd were Muslims nursing their tea for two hours and talking passionately amongst themselves about something you might never figure. Patrick ventured that the subject matter of their heated exchange was probably something as mundane as the cost of tea in China.

By the end of their shift (this scene blew away the movies), Jitka, Michal and I were joined by Lada and his girl to smoke a big fat joint on the balcony. They were off to U Sudu to play fotbalek (foosball) and invited me to join them.

This began my adventures in the underground of Prague, which belongs to the extraordinary youth of the Czech Republic. Dreadlocked or punked out, studious or Bohemian, they were the finest group of youngsters I'd ever encountered. And these kids knew how to enjoy themselves without getting shitfaced. I suppose their parents had figured out a few centuries ago that as long as they took care of their school or their work or whatever they needed to do, why shouldn't they hang out at their pubs and have a few, while Mom and Dad were at theirs' across the street?

U Sudu (wine bar) was a labyrinth of descending tunnels and cavernous rooms built in 1456 or something. Each level down got smokier and stinkier, with everybody sharing joints, drinking beer, watching videos, bouncing from table to table, shouting over reggae and rock.

Foreigners in the know were scattered about and fotbalek was being played by all in earnest. Now here was a sport that I could really get into. I knew of no other where: 1) The girls could be as good as the guys on a consistent basis (their sound effects were much cooler too, as they crescendoed to the orgasm of the score). 2) Anyone halfway decent could beat anyone really good in any given game. 3) It was way more fun to play doubles (further supporting #2) and 4) Partaking in a big fat joint just before your turn came up was actually an advantage. No fouls, no cheating, no off-sides, no bullies, no ball hogs. A time out after every score. What a game. I sucked so bad that everyone wanted to play with me.

The Drunken Tourist

We then took the #9 Tram up to Prague 4, the neighborhood known as Zizkoff. We hit Nad Viktorkou, a modest looking bar from the outside, but then through the back it opened up to a whole other bar under the chestnut trees. Nobody cared at all about the smoke and rock n' roll was blasting with the fotbalek again, this time in the open air. They even had an out of tune piano in the corner that I smashed on along with the tunes being piped in. I don't recall noticing a juke-box the whole time I was in town.

The beer garden on top of Narodny must have had twenty tables, all outside, some under tents, with youngsters milling from table to table, drinking Pivo (beer) and smoking spliffs (spliffs) under the stars. The view looked down on the city in three directions for miles and the crowd was in a real holiday spirit. After all, it was Monday or Tuesday, and the work of the day was ancient history.

At about ten we hit Akropolis for reggae night. I met Cooper and Jules and Billy from Canada, Sean and Josh from Australia, Dave and his sister from Ireland, all of them current residents, some of them for years. Jules and Billy were teaching English, working with private students as well as corporations. Dave was acting and almost paying his rent, mostly as an extra. Sean and Josh had a band and worked in the bars. It seemed like everyone was pretty much broke, living the high life. Except for Cooper. Cooper was just bumming around, living the highest life of all. Everybody liked this guy and it looked like he knew everybody. He probably hadn't paid for a beer in six months. It just didn't seem proper for him to do so.

Our DJ was rapping it up over the reggae, sweating it out with all of us on the dance floor. I was bumping into ripped representatives from all over the map. It was a stone-cold happy riot in full swing. We were on top of our game, on top of that hill, in the center of the center of the free world – Zizkoff in Praha!

* * *

Five days later my package had arrived at Jana's. With shipping the film worked out to a buck a shot. If I charged a hundred Krones a shot that would be cheap, even for this town – less than the cost of two good beers at a tourist spot. If I took 12 good shots a day I had my rent. This was not including tips. I also had to figure freebies and pictures that didn't come out.

"Excuse me sir, you seem to be having a wonderful time tonight. Would you like a souvenir photo?" would work as a good opener for Mishka, the perfect partner for this schtick. "Yes, yes, this is a good spot here. The light is good, very good," I would add in that spanking new Americanese of mine. "You two should have a souvenir together, yes? Kristoff is very good photo-grapher," Mishka might add. She was, how you say in English? She was 'money', yes?

People seemed to like the novelty. Anyone could take a picture, but a souvenir photograph by Kristoff, capturing a magical night of love in Prague, developed before your eyes? Now that was a whole different story.

We would come back around to see how it came out and ask if they wanted another one. Mishka must have approached 200 couples that first night. It was certainly the hardest part of the gig and she couldn't care less what people thought or how they brushed us off. There was no way I could have done it alone. She even convinced three different Czech managers that this was good for their café business, and she was right. Getting paid for 17 photographs, we used up 20 shots and had a ball. I drank liberally through the evening and we shared a good meal. Mishka took home almost double what she made at the sunglass hut on a good day. I would have been more than happy if I broke even with my share. The folks I thought would be duds turned out to be the coolest. Only one guy ended up really yelling at us not to dare take his picture. We figured he was pretending to be somebody to impress everybody. We were not concerned. Our mood was too good and it proved contagious. Prague was a very innocent, spontaneous city to me, despite its noble history and despite the mass commercialism currently attacking that history. And where else could a guy like Kristoff find work?

* * *

Then I got sick. Really sick. I had exhausted myself on account of the drink. The next two days were spent in bed sweating out mind and body. In between waking up and forcing myself back to sleep, I was second guessing myself as only an insecure egomaniac of my stature could. I would feel awful about what I was doing, then

The Drunken Tourist

feel great about what I was doing. What nonsense. Experience had proved that this type of thinking was not to be taken seriously. So I read and listened to the BBC. I took hot baths and drank a lot of water. Simple stuff. No big deals. Soon enough I woke up again in the middle of Europe.

I had begun to inquire about Berlin more than a week ago, but hadn't found anyone that could give me any good leads to follow. One guy had drawn me a lame map and had recommended a hostel. That was it. Still, I was ready to move as soon as I could get my energy back. I pictured the town to be wet and cooler with a sophisticated night life. I was hoping to find some players there. Here in Prague, I couldn't find anyone to sit in with me. Furthermore, the communication level with my associates had settled on this very thin plateau, especially with the girls. I mean, how often can you say, "look, how beautiful," and not elaborate? I certainly was not, as the Beatles tune kept playing, "deep in love, without a lot to say," and neither were they. I missed my Queen, refusing to accept that she was back home with her own "ticket to ride, and she don't care."

That evening I settled my account with Jana. With a lot less drinking and a lot more work, I could have almost broke even for the whole time I was in town. Considering what I actually spent, I lived like a king.

Jana had converted her place into a boarding house two years ago after her husband had passed away. You could tell she was still very lonely. She was really a decent woman. I admired her quiet reserve. She didn't seem to judge me too harshly on the drink and the girls, either. She appreciated how I kept my trail as I found it. We had come a long way from where we first met. I mentioned my dad's passing, so we got into that a little, reminiscing on what long suffering men her husband and my dad were over a bottle of vodka she had in the freezer. I couldn't believe that bottle had been in there the whole time.

She ironed my blue suit, white shirt and gold tie before I headed down the hill, planning on finally going to the outdoor opera. Verdi was on the bill and I was late. I waited across the square and enjoyed my twilight town until intermission. Back in New York, I used to see the second half of Broadway shows all the time by dressing well and waiting for the break. Either the ushers would let me in with everyone else or I'd pull the old ticket stub routine. This worked well at Lincoln Center, too. At rock concerts the stakes were higher and security tougher, but if I wanted it bad enough, I would eventually get in somehow.

This all went true to form tonight as well, but the Opera wasn't the best and I was restless. I tried to get into it, but I have to admit, I wasn't all there. Mentally, I had already left town.

Berlin

The day had started out well enough. I had made it to Hlvani Station back in Prague early that morning. The timetable board was simple to understand and the ticket to Berlin worked out to something like fifty bucks. I decided to pay the fare and save the day on my Euralpass. The train ride was simply beautiful. Mountain passes with steep grades straight down to the river, wide open views of the countryside, the whole works. I shared the six seat compartment with Jonathan from Liverpool. When I entered, he had a book by Jean-Paul Sartre lying open on the empty seat next to him. By the way he dressed you could guess right off he was something of a Deadhead. The fact that he was in Medical School wasn't so easily recognizable. He was off to Amsterdam to meet two of his University buddies for one last blowout for the summer before hunkering down into school again. When he asked me how Prague was, the word "grand" kept coming up. He expressed some remorse for not being able to explore the city more extensively.

"I know how you feel," I said. "The disappointments hardest to bear are those which never come."

"Excuse me?" he said. "Could you repeat that?"

"The disappointments hardest to bear are those which never come. How about I write it down for you?"

"That would be great."

"It's not my line," I said, "but it is one of my favorites." I left it at that.

"What's it from?"

"It's from the Morontia Mota in the Urantia Book. In fact a few readers I know are big fans of your pal Jean-Paul over there. They like to find comparisons within the texts."

"Well," he said, "I'd like to check it out sometime. What was the name of the book again?"

"It's called the Urantia Book. I've got a copy on me. I'll dig it up later and we can trade for a while."

"Sure thing," he said. I liked how neither one of us pressed. We hit it off so well together I guess we didn't want to ruin the mood with too much, too soon. Now if I could only adopt this attitude toward women. Unfortunately, I was way too desperate for all that. We each went back to our books respectively, had a cold one, admired the scenery and discussed our itineraries. This fellow was the genuine article – ambition and respect. He lit up when I told him my plans included Barcelona. Immediately he offered the address of a boarding house there that proved valuable down the road. I asked him to draw me a rough guide of Barcelona that included his highlights. My man took to the task with delight.

"Could I take a look at that Sartre while you're at it?" I asked.

"By all means," he replied, a little too maturely. After a while, I took out The Urantia Book and began to cross reference with the Sartre in hand. I opened to page 556, read one or two Motas, then laid the book out on the seat next to mine.

"Is that the book you were talking about?" he inquired.

"Yeah," I said without looking up. "It's open to the pages with that quote, check it out if you like." I added casually, "man, this Sartre is heavy… how long have you been reading this book?"

"It's my second time through it," he said proudly as he reached for mine. At that point I felt safely past one of those tricky introductions where I'd have to say something like, "Well, Urantia happens to be the name of our planet as far as the rest of the inhabited spheres are concerned."

It was so much simpler to find a groove in someone else's spirituality than to lay all that on them all at once. Jonathan was obviously easier to approach than most. Try telling a fundamentalist that you've got hundreds of pages here on the life and teachings of Jesus written by celestial beings who watched the whole drama unfold from on high.

By the time the train was on the outskirts of Berlin, Jonathan had given me his email address and was psyched to get to the Urantia Book website. He then invited me to go straight away to Amsterdam

The Drunken Tourist

with him. He had good friends there who would welcome me to stay with them. This was awfully tempting. After all, I was relying on serendipity for a travel agent. It would be very simple to stay on the train and go back to Berlin next week. Then again, once in Amsterdam, I'd probably want to head for Paris. We said our goodbyes just as the train pulled into Bahnhof Zoo Station. The decision had been made courtesy of the quote that introduced us.

* * *

My plan was simple. Head to East Berlin first and find a cheap bed for the night. The next day I could walk around, hands free, devoted to finding a great deal on lodging for the week. It was awfully hot and muggy as I waited for the S-Bahn train. Maybe this town was like New York after all.

I had visions of the East Village as I made my way to East Berlin. Yeah right. Alexanderplatz reminded me of Yonkers. Excuse me, dat's Yankus to most evry bhady from Yankus. I got off ova 'dere in Alexanderplatz 'cause I like da name. So fuckin' sue me, alright? The only spot around that looked cool was the Television Tower. I figyad from up 'dere over here, I could get a betta' idea where ta go ova'dere ova'here.

From the top of the tower I saw a sprawling metropolis with no definable center. The whole city seemed to be under construction. The skyline was littered with cranes in every direction. I wondered briefly how they could afford all of this then headed back to the station stop. I asked someone for a good place to get off of the train for what I was looking for. His response was something like, "I live here; why would I know where to find transient lodging?"

For the rest of the afternoon I walked the streets of East Berlin, feeling ridiculous in my silver suit, dragging my big bag behind me, sweating it out. Still I kept rolling, kept asking stupid questions, and kept getting nowhere.

Deciding it was a bad day to try to stay sober, I stopped for a beer at a local skinhead bar, considering it seemed to be the cheapest place to get a beer around. You know they were loving my action. I might have been a tad overdressed for the occasion. I might have been a tad overcharged for the beer, too. By the tone of the looks coming my way, they must have been thinking, "Who is this freakin' guy anyway, thinking he's all that in his monkey suit, looking for a cheap place to stay. I'll give him a cheap place to stay all right. Come to think of it, there might be a vacancy in that real cozy elevator shaft just a few short blocks from here." I felt like Pee Wee on his big adventure.

The cheapest place I found with an open bed was about sixty bucks for the night. No thank you; it wasn't even dark yet. Back on the S-Train, I went all the way back to Zoo Station and started over. That's when I got directed to the Tourist Information office at the Europa Center next to the Kaiser Wilhelm Gedachtniskirche right down the Kurfurstendamm. From there, I was directed to go to the Jugendg-asthaus am Zoo. That would be pronounced You-gund-gawst-house ahm Zoo. It was located a few blocks down from the station I had just come from on Hardenbergstrasse (pronounced Hardenbergstrasse). It was also called the JGH Hostel. I mean alright already with the houseandstreudelnoodlebagel.

Reneé was in town from Vienna on holiday from a semester at the University there. His English was much better than the Australian fellows who were sharing the room with us. He dressed much better too. We introduced ourselves by listening to each other's music. Reneé sounded like Lou Reed as a young immigrant from Russia. He took the comparison as a major compliment. We headed out straightaway to find a cheap place to eat and drink. The beers at the restaurant worked out to five bucks each and a plate of pasta was ten. We both wanted substantially more than our budget would allow at that rate. Neither one of us were in the mood to travel far to find an affordable Kneipe, so we shopped at the local market down the street. We split a bottle of fruit syrup and mixed it with the cheap beer back at the bar in the hostel. The Weissbier mit Schuss concocted pretty much sucked, but I got a lot out of our emotional conversation. After bitching for a while about our latest romantic disasters we were inevitably stuck with having to wrap it up before things got too sappy. I think we were mostly motivated by how downright uncool it would have been to just sit there as another pair of commiserating, lovesick losers. If anything, we needed a little resolution just to lose the pesky neon sign now tattooed on our foreheads that clearly read to any female within

The Drunken Tourist

a mile as, "Hi there beautiful; we're desperately on holiday."

Reneé then gave me a critical piece of information that would wear on me down the road like a denim jacket. "My feelings are my own," he said simply. "No one can take them away from me." Now this might be common knowledge for most folks, but for an emotionally handicapped guy like me, this was direct revelation. Furthermore, the way he said it was almost as impressive as what he said. Even his posture improved as he elaborated, "You know, come to think of it, I'm still living with all that love I was able to give her." It didn't matter to him that the degree of giving might have been lopsided. In fact, it had worked out to his advantage. Again he restated his point, "I just loved to love this woman." That much he could live with. The details were a separate issue. He had recycled the wreckage and come up big in the process.

At first, this line of reasoning sounded too selfless for me to buy. Then I had to consider the alternative. All I was doing was cursing my girl because I hurt more than she did. Since the sacred formula of our chemistry had been violated, she was the guilty one because she was the one able to move on so easily. I would take this thinking so far that I would fantasize about the day the light would come on in her deepest despair. She would cry out, "If only I had stayed with him – how could I have strayed from such a love?" And there I would be with my benevolent hard-on, imposing a suspended sentence now that she had seen the error of her ways.

The following day we decided to hop on a local bus and find the Berlin we were both looking for. We had the names of a few streets recommended and a city bus map, confident we'd have an easy go of it considering at least one of us spoke German. We lasted three, maybe four stops. It was way too hot and crowded to ride any public transportation anywhere for fun, with or without an interpreter.

We ended up back at the square around the Kaiser Wilhelm Church. I just loved that bombed out church. Reneé wasn't as impressed. He was enjoying what was going on around it. I didn't care for it much at all. It reminded me of Washington Square Park in New York with less women, more tourists and only two performers that day. The first act was two people in leotards sort of balancing each other. The guy was on his back with his feet in the air supporting the girl from her stomach with her arms outstretched as they attempted to get her to do a full circle with him moving his feet on her belly. Ta-Dahh! Big fucking deal. They actually got dressed up for this? We used to call it a Flying Angel when I did it when my kid was a baby to distract him long enough so he would stop crying. O.K., so they made it all the way around a little more smoothly. They were professionals, after all.

The other act was a one man band playing "Stairway to Heaven" while his hat lit up when his foot went down to beat his drum. What got me was the circle of adoring youngsters sitting Indian style around this fella looking up at him in such reverence. Wasn't this the same Zoo Station that U2 named an album after? Reneé figured it must be a different scene once the sun went down. I agreed and related my experience in Prague that supported this theory.

Meanwhile, we both didn't want to be caught dead around there so we just tripped around looking for an affordable place to eat. The day just wasn't going our way. There's always those days when you've just got to settle for nothing bad happening, especially on the road.

The best deal in town turned out to be renting a bicycle for the day. By the time we got around to finding the bike stand, the vendor only had the female style available. This presented the opportunity to negotiate. We haggled the price down to what amounted to twelve bucks each for the rest of the day. I gave the guy my dummy debit card and my expired driver's license for the deposit. Once we got past the initial gayness of riding on a red woman's bicycle advertising a chain of wiener stands, we really started to enjoy ourselves. The routes of the city were extremely well organized and efficient despite the major overhaul taking place. This kind of renovation in New York or L.A. would have resulted in a complete standstill and a dramatic rise in the crime rate.

We cruised through Tiergarten Park, made our way to the Brandenburg Gate, then past the Berlin Wall to Museum Island. It was all very impressive and well put together. I don't know why I felt so far removed. Overall we were having a decent afternoon. The only bitch was that we couldn't lock up our bikes.

That evening we went back to Zoo Station and Reneé was right. The

The Drunken Tourist

place was different. There were more policemen, more young men from the Middle East getting busted for selling hash, and the one man band's hat looked a whole lot better lighting up at night.

I came to the conclusion that it would take a good amount of time and money to properly get to know this town. I had played with the idea of submitting my tunes to a few German record labels while I was in Berlin, most notably the label that carried Nick Cave and the Bad Seeds. Reneé was all for it. Then again, I had a couple of years on him and knew the kind of effort it realistically takes to get anywhere with any label. Truthfully, I just didn't feel like getting into the whole thing. I told him I was on sabbatical from the results business and the time necessary was not on the itinerary.

My friend had decided earlier to leave by checkout time the next day, so I figured it was time for me to go, too. I would have to leave town without finding the beat of Berlin I was looking for. Maybe it was out there for me, maybe not. I could live with either. I had seen some of the sights, avoided any problems, and was moving on. Maybe sometimes that was the best you could ask for. I couldn't expect the kind of luck I had in Prague everywhere I went. I told myself that my heart had embraced a real souvenir that "nobody could take away from me." Not without a fight, anyway. With that I could leave feeling a little more emotionally stable. There would be other hands dealt on other days.

"That's it," my heart assured me. "It just wasn't in the cards."

FERRY
MARVELOUS
CENTRAL
STATION
INFO
DOCKS
CAFES
TROLLEYS
TOO
CIVILIZED
NEIGHBORHOOD
EXCHANGE
HASH
SHIT
COKE & SPEED
SMOKE COKE
FAT HOOKERS
TELEPHONES
HOSTEL
CANAL
HOSTELS
REDLIGHT
NICE VIEW
LION
DOCKS
AMSTERDAM
CAFES
JORDAAN
HOSTEL
CREPES
CREPES
CREPES
DAM
SQUARE
COKE
BARS
SEX
COFFEE HOUSES
BARS
HOSTELS
COFFEE HOUSE
$100
BEER
SMOKE
HOOKERS
OBVIOUS
GAY
HASH
CANALS
PIZZA
DANCE
HEINEKEN
CRACKHOUSE
BIKE PATHS
CANAL
BIKE PATH
GOOD
DUCK
ATLAS
BIKE PATHS
CANALS
SWEET
SPOT
CANALS
RIJKS
MUSEUM
PARK
VAN GOGH
MUSEUM
PARK
BEAUTIES ON BIKES
TROLLEY
BIKE PATHS
TROLLEYS
LOVELY HOOD

Amsterdam

From the minute I stepped off the train, I knew Amsterdam was a circus. It looked all dressed up like a pretty little whore with no underwear on. Centraal Station was truly central station. Everybody surrounding the building was sprawled out all over the pavement. Long hairs with backpacks everywhere. Indians and Africans selling you-name-it, you-need-it. Youngsters bumming change with no shame. A teenage Deadhead and her puppy approached me for a dollar for dog food. There was even the guy with the monkey and the cart playing the wind-up song.

The view ahead of me was downright psychedelic. The line at the tourist information booth was half a mile long and for me to buy a map would be ridiculous. Everybody spoke English anyway, so why not just walk in the direction everybody else was walking? By the time I negotiated the three minute stroll to Dam Square, I was approached at least ten times by someone selling some kind of drug or some kind of phone card. This town made New York City look like Orange County on a Sunday morning. Even the metal cones that separated the sidewalk from the street were shaped like slick dicks with ribbed condoms on.

From the square I was directed to walk down the Zeedijk to look for a hostel. There was bar after bar after bar along the crowded narrow street that I chose on my quest to ditch my luggage. Then there was a bar and a coffee house then another coffee house then a sex shop then another coffee house and then there she was – my first look at a hooker in a window. This woman was gigantic, Asian, and unashamed. She was sitting on a tall chair, turned around like your teacher used to do during those heart to hearts before the whip came down. Her red bikini was almost completely enveloped in her rolls of flesh flapping freely. The thighs were enormous, her toe nails bright red and twitching around in anticipation. The smile she flashed was actually quite nice and she had almost all her teeth.

The men around me were kidding each other to go on and take a turn. I thought that maybe one of them would be back after he ditched his pals and went out on his own. I don't know why, but the whole scene made me want to run to the nearest Catholic Church.

With no church in sight, I found the cheapest bar I could find in the immediate neighborhood. I ordered a beer and the bartender handed me a menu. There were pictures of different buds of exotic marijuana alongside grams of hashish, each with a price that had been changed often. The whole menu was really cute. On the bar was a pie tray with a "space cake" sold by the slice and baked with hash or reefer. If I had been a true stoner, I would have been drooling.

I asked a few people if they could recommend a hostel nearby. Good luck. No one was going out of their way except maybe to go to the bathroom. What really got me was that no one was smiling. You figure everybody would be having this outrageously extroverted good time, but it wasn't like that at all. Most everyone was paired up or in little groups at the tables, keeping to themselves and concentrating on the whole smoking procedure. Maybe it was the terrible music the bar was playing. I got myself fortified on another brew and moved on, looking for a place to stay and a smile on the street. Still the neighborhood countenance was grim, despite all the flashy signs and window dressings. My old 1.5 second rule was being violated with relish. Who knows, maybe the exchange of a smile around here would have to infer the exchange of some sex.

I eventually found a bed at the Bull Dog Hostel, right in the middle of the Red Light district. I checked into a room that featured one window and maybe twenty bunk beds in two rows on each side of the room. Young men cocooning for their ensuing smokefest later that evening were currently occupying more than half the beds. It was depressing. I didn't have a padlock for my assigned locker so I immediately went back downstairs and begged the front desk clerk to

The Drunken Tourist

keep my big bag locked up in the office. There was a sign at the desk that read "Midget Hookers/Half Price".

I left all my valuables locked up in the hostel safe except for my wallet and my spending cash. This part of town was full of junkies and thieves, that was a given. Who knows what the current market value was for an American passport and the rest of my collection. I dressed way down in my black trench and hit the streets looking like your average junkie thief on holiday.

After scarfing down a falafel, I bought a pint of Bourbon at the liquor store for my twilight stroll around the district. I noticed there were no unescorted women anywhere. Go figure. This mecca was designed for the male pleasure seeker, no doubt about that.

The best coffee shop I found was on an old boat tied up along one of the canals toward the fringe of the district. I walked down the galley into a smoke filled room with pictures of buds framed on the wall and a glass case of pipes that was used as the bar. I bought ten bucks worth of hash and took a table on the deck. It didn't bother me that no alcohol was being served– my old pal Jack was kicking in quite nicely, thank you. The tables around me filled up with hippies on holiday and local young professionals with their cell phones and newspapers, ready for their evening smoke. The art of the smoke was obviously taken very seriously around here. And of course, the roll was most critical. The hash was heated a little with a lighter so it crumbled easily into a fair pile of tobacco in the palm of the designated roller's hand. A tiny cardboard cylinder from a matchbook cover was waiting along with a double long rolling paper. The paper was placed over the pile of tobacco and hash before the critical flip of the palms that were held together in prayer. The paper was now full for the consequent roll. With any luck, the joint would develop into a fluted affair and before a good lick, the tiny cardboard filter would be shoved in the narrow end just as the deal was sealed. Survey says… 9.60. What a procedure. Now all you had to do was smoke it properly.

Most people smoked it like somebody would smoke a cigarette right after they had spent a weekend in jail. At least two, usually three hits before the pass. The correct pass itself also seemed to be socially imperative. The smoker would hold his last hit in while the joint was

held high and vertical for inspection as if to say, "You see what a refined smoker I am? It is still burning beautifully." Only after a suave
exchange would the exhale surface, if things went true to form.

I imitated the roll and the smoke all by my lonesome. I never
could figure out how cannabis relaxed people. It usually made me hy-
persensitive. A couple of hits and I'd be internally frantic for hours. I
just couldn't handle the stuff. Today was no exception. This hash had
to be twice as strong as anything I had smoked in a long time. Yet I
hung in there at the dope boat until the sun went down, alternating
between waves of introspection slapping me around and spells of just
sitting there alone at my table… wondering what everyone thought
of me, just sitting there alone at my table.

Achtung Baby snapped me out of it. The Edge's guitar roared
through my lull with *The Real Thing* reminding me of how fortunate
I really was. This was by far my favorite U2, full of melody and message without the posturing anthems. "Thank you God," I thought.
"You always give me the full experience. There's a whole world
about… let's go look around some more."

The world of food was more like it. I started with an excellent
slice of pizza, then took the French Fries with mayonnaise to go.
Before the fries were gone I was looking over a smorgasbord at some
Indonesian restaurant with a gigantic plate of Rijstafel. This dish had
it all except the fat hooker in the window. I'm thinking, "What good
are these napkins anyway, napkins are silly, I'm just going to have to
use another one later." Nothing was missed along the gorge-out until
I discovered crepes filled with something like Nutella. "Ohh baby!
There is no longer any need for me to look any further for any other
flavor. I will be yours forever. I admit, the Marzipan may tempt me,
but this is it. I'll never stray." The Nutella crepe got me. I was asleep
back in my bunk in half an hour.

* * *

Day two in Amsterdam found me well rested, having coffee and a
crepe at a bistro along a canal, no Nutella in sight. Today I wanted
to get out of my slicks and into an old pair of jeans. There had to
be a few thrift stores in this town that seemed to sell everything. My
quest took me all the way to the other side of the train station, past

The Drunken Tourist

four or five major canals, to an area they called the Jordaan, known for its art galleries. When I arrived however, it was clear; there would be no thrift stores here. "Vintage," sure, but certainly no thrift. The area reminded me of a couple of blocks in Soho that I used to wander through, wondering how all these artists I never heard of could afford to live there. Still, it was a welcome change from the all out barrage of decadence I had just come from. Being surrounded by all that "sinnin'" was fundamentally fucking with my sex drive.

On the way back to the station I put on my best art connoisseur pose and prepared to window shop the current masterpieces. A Manet and two Lautrec's greeted me with their coy smiles. A Modigliani and a Matisse vied for my attention in a more subtle play. One Gauguin just stood there, refusing eye contact as I turned a corner into the Louvre of all whorehouses. Picasso's blue, pink, African and even Cubist styles were all well represented here. Renoir and deKooning had a curious tag team going on in the last booth. The Italians of the Renaissance were curiously absent, but down the street the Oriental influence was competing with the whole Eastern Bloc, out in full force. I was a long way from home.

There was a ferry that left every ten or fifteen minutes from behind the train station. It was a short commuter route to what might be considered a borough or suburb of Amsterdam. I stayed on the boat for two round trips. Besides the diversity of the phenomenal waterfront, it simply felt good moving along surrounded by water. On the second trip, I smoked a hastily rolled hash joint (maybe a 5.5 on the coffee shop scorecard considering the degree of difficulty) and actually enjoyed the high. Everything was moving along in fine order from where I was sitting.

Leaning over the railing I even ventured an old tune:

> *I've been a sailor on that sea of heartbreak*
> *I am a sailor now that seeks no shore*
> *Out here the wind and the waves take hold of fate*
> *Out here you deal with what's dealt no more.*
> *It's true… Almost too good… And it's all here for the asking*
> *Ridin' them waves with the breeze,*

Santana

can't come back till I made it
All the way around... go on... hang the doubt
I'm rolling all the way... Why worry now?

By the time I crossed the first bridge to the left past Centraal Station, I was approached three times to buy coke. These guys were obviously too bold to have anything real. Although cannabis maximus was encouraged around here, cocaine and the rest of the hard stuff carried with it stiff sentences.

The next guy solicited me with that look that I was all too familiar with. I broke down and asked for a taste. He asked me if I was police. This I took as a good sign. Still, it was garbage. I waved him off and walked on. About twenty yards ahead, a guy on foot pulled up and whispered, "Hey man, hey man." I just kept walking without looking his way.

"Hey man, I saw you blow that guy off back there, what are you looking for?"

"Nothing," I said, and continued without breaking stride.

"Look man, I ain't no cop and if you want something real I can get it, but we have to travel for it. You're not going to find anything real around here. I'm not into jackin' you, I just want to get high."

"Where did you pick up that expression?"

"What expression?"

"That you're not into jackin' me."

"I guess I picked it up in the States last year, down in D.C."

"Alright then, let's keep walking."

"You're not a cop, are you?"

"No, I'm not a cop and you're not a cop, so let's not attract any cops, O.K.?"

Tom Paul was certainly not a cop. He was a nice fellow with a wife waiting at home with their five year old son. He just happened to have this little habit of smoking crack. He also had a pretty nice late model Audi which we drove to an apartment building about fifteen minutes away.

On the second floor there was a room with about seven guys and three ladies all seated hunched over a table in the middle of the room. Nobody even looked up as our host led us into the back of the apart-

The Drunken Tourist

ment. A gram of powder was fifty bucks and we would be cooking it right there on the spot. Tom Paul took charge by dumping the whole gram in a small glass bottle that had a bit of water and a little baking soda in it. I was never any good at this, so I just hung out checking up on the group in the living room, hoping none of them would come in and beg for a hit. The dirty deed was done in no time, producing a chunk the size of a replacement eraser you stick on a pencil.

All anybody had to use for a pipe was a metal hash pipe, or else a home made number with tin foil for a screen. I wondered out loud why nobody had glass pipes around here. Either no one understood me or nobody was giving up theirs. My heart was racing and I could have shit right there just before I took that first hit. OO0hhh buddy, that first hit. Suspended in the swoosh. Didn't have to think. The blast completely wiped out everything but the feeling. All my attention was absorbed in some greedy type of mind and body erection.

The initial euphoria lasted less than ten seconds. My first thought was the second hit. Yes, it was on, and yes I had more. I did another double hit immediately and held it in a little longer. Lust battled greed for thinking rights. I had to pass the pipe to Tom Paul for his turn. He should have gotten his own. I looked around and nothing had changed. I was surprised nobody was crowding around me for a hit. Didn't these girls know I was in the room with a fistful of crack? They had their own and they didn't care. Quite a change from the crack houses in L.A. where you're obligated to give some up for the house and people would crowd you for a crumb – wouldn't let you enjoy your high, much less let you come down in peace. Lord, I hate coming down.

I wrestled the emergency fifty from my wallet and gave it to my new partner without saying a word. I wasn't going to wait until I ran out to get more. Like I said, it was on. I tried to snuggle my way into the group at the table but no one was the least bit interested in me joining them. Like I said, they all had theirs. Well fine, I thought, I'll take another hit and go. Then again, I really don't want to run around town like this. So I'll take one more hit besides that one and then go. Maybe it really was time to go, or maybe it would be worse outside. I might just want to take another hit before it's too late. Too late for what? Too late not to be all tweaked-out in the drug capitol of the world.

Santana

My new partner maintained his cool long enough to finally get me out the door and back into his car. I got out of there with about half of the second batch left to smoke. He unceremoniously dropped me off where he picked me up, promising to look me up tomorrow. I was left alone, me and my monster, loose on the streets of Sin City. I had to find a liquor store to down a few flaming gulps in an attempt to stabilize. That worked on me just long enough to make me jones for another hit. I went into a coffeehouse bathroom and loaded up my little contraption with a sizable blast. I fired it up and held it in all the way back out the door and into the street. "Oh buddy, now there ya go," I told myself as I let the cloud fly, "everybody is stoned; nobody cares." So why couldn't I shake the tweak long enough to even re- motely enjoy my high?

If I went back to the hostel, I'd have to stay in. The curfew was two a.m., so that wouldn't work; it was only midnight. I defi- nitely did not want to be stuck tossing and turning around with my bunkies all night. So I kept walking, glasses on, avoiding any eye contact along with the rest of the throng. The ladies in the windows were somehow looking a whole lot better this evening. This one thin blonde in particular could probably use a hit off the pipe for a change. "Forget about it," I told myself. "This hooker could owe a cop a favor and I could get busted right there behind the curtain." I didn't have enough money or any real interest in the whole business anyway. Probably wouldn't have even got hard. Maybe I just felt a need to share. When I found a stairwell off an alley, I did the last of it and threw the pipe to the ground before I let the rest of the evidence hit the atmosphere. Now I could finally enjoy my high. Yeah right.

Up ahead I saw that the Big Top was in town. They had the lions in a cage behind a barricade along the outside of the circus tent. The female was sleeping and the male was pacing. He caught site of me and froze, staring directly at me. I returned the favor. After thirty seconds I was convinced this was some kind of super- natural showdown. Onlookers gathered to watch this test of wills transpire. This lion would not move, would not be distracted. We just kept looking at each other. I don't know if the audience thought this was a warm-up act to attract customers or what. Neither one of us budged. His stare said: "You are going against the laws of

The Drunken Tourist

the universe, these laws of nature that I represent." I glared back, silently insisting: "This state I am in is part of my experience that you are trying to fathom." My argument was weak but my resolve fierce. From the corner of my eye I could see people trying to get a look at me. I might as well have been in an iron cage of my own. The female started to show signs of waking but still my man held firm. All I know is that we kept up our eye contact longer than it took three separate crowds to take turns observing us at the barricade. Finally he roared right at my face and turned completely around. He had enough of me. I felt eaten alive.

What could I do but walk away? I felt all itchy, wanting to jump into the nearest canal. Instead I kept walking as loneliness hit home. I couldn't look up to my God. Time was a bitch coming down long and hard. Guilty again, crashing and spinning, wanting back to the land of the living. My walk was stiff with hands taut in the pockets of my coat as I zigzagged my way over stone bridges. The neighborhoods turned quieter walking away from the city center. Whenever there was a dead end, I would turn around and circle back well enough not to lose all sense of direction. I made bold to invite any celestial allies that I hadn't completely pissed off to share some mileage. The drugs were starting to wear off.

It was still dark when I came upon the monstrous silhouette of the Rijks Museum. I silently saluted the beasts at the entrance then turned the corner to find a park on the north side of the building. Over the fence was a grove of pines hiding a few wooden benches cornering the path. I curled up in my black trench and asked God for sleep or not.

* * *

Morning found me alive and well. Downright perky, considering. Back over the fence there were two middle aged artists setting up their paintings for sale against the railing on the sidewalk. Down the way there was a sweet looking blonde maneuvering her hot dog cart into position for the day. Smiling faces were zipping by on bicycles built for two. The streets looked spotless and the town house gardens were in summer bloom. I must have woke up in a different city.

Santana

Before the entrance to the Rijks, I noticed a sign with an arrow pointing toward the Van Gogh Museum down the street. This stop had been a definite on my agenda when I first took the train into town. Now it was right here waiting and I didn't have a dime on me. By the time I pulled up, the line at the ticket window must have been thirty deep.

The exit was guarded by one fellow in uniform stationed next to a second door in. He saw me coming towards him with my best, "I'm bewildered" look. I took out my wallet without breaking stride and by the time we were face to face, I had a picture of my son in my hand.

"Excuse me please, sir," I said without panic, "you see this boy? He may have come out this way… did you notice, please?" I stuck the picture towards his face.

"No sir," he answered. "Not out this door here, sir."

"Is there another exit, please?" I asked as I looked around.

"No sir," he replied, "he may have gone out the front, but this is the exit here only."

"Well," I answered with a casual shrug, "he must be on the second floor with his mom. I should go this way to look, yes?" He let me pass without a second thought.

Van Gogh's "Almond Blossoms" was waiting on the second floor. That blue was all over me. I was finally swimming. The brush work was flatter than what I expected but the intensity was all there. The blue was vibrating against the white buds of the branches just reaching out far enough. How could this guy possibly second guess himself? And what would a good woman in his life have done for his work? Good, bad, or indifferent? Well, doubtfully indifferent.

Somewhere between one of the artist's nervous breakdowns, I made it to the first floor cafeteria. There was a long line behind the cashier's station and the self-service parade was backed up to the beginning of the metal railing that supported the trays.

I stocked up on fruit and sandwiches and chose a local red wine to compliment my breakfast. Towards the end of the food display cases I made up my mind that I had forgotten something at the beginning of the line, retreating back that direction and out the entrance to the seating area. I would explain that I was being courteous, if I had to. It seemed like every museum in the world had one of these cafeterias

The Drunken Tourist

selling four day old tuna fish sandwiches for six bucks. Besides, old Vinny wouldn't mind, that's for sure.

Back on my feet, I continued to have the best experience at a museum that I could remember. The power of the work was infectious. Everyone was absorbed and respectful except for two or three idiots with their video cameras recording for all posterity what they were missing right there in front of them for all posterity. No dummy with a lens was going to bully this view while I was around. We little folk stood firm and the spell was not broken.

After one thorough round I needed a smoke. On the way out the in door, I signaled to the ticket taker I would be right back by holding up a cigarette. She waved me on and might have said not to worry.

I lit up and looked around optimistically. People were having their smoke, absorbed in some reading material or sunning themselves with their eyes closed and their feet dangling over the concrete wall at the front of the building.

There were quite a few beautiful ladies around, but I didn't bother any of them – didn't want to risk compromising any bit of the fine mood we all seemed to be in. Even the staff seemed happy to be working. And all of this was being brought to us care of Mr. Van Gogh. Talk about a guy ahead of his time. On the way back in I hailed my patron at the exit door to let him know all was well. I don't think he even remembered me.

The trolley back towards the center of town displayed a serene city. The cafes were packed with businessmen drinking Heinekens while blondes on bicycles kept up with the train. We passed rows of old brick townhouses with well kept gardens that made up perfect blocks. I entertained the thought of how sweet it would be to live here with my lover. I left the train near the entrance to a beautifully manicured park. Fifty yards in, I found a spot on the grass and nodded off in the sun.

The train to Paris left every night at 23:00 (11:00 p.m.). Depending on whether there was a bed at the Bull Dog, I could stay or I could go. I certainly didn't relish the idea of traipsing around with my luggage looking for another bed. The Gay Games had arrived in town making a good night's sleep even harder to come by. I went back to find my lion but the Big Top was rolling it up and moving on.

DIVER

MUSEUM (CLOSED) BLVD.

THEATRE

ARC

HORRISON

MONTPARNASSE

VISITOR

RIDICULOUS GROCERY STORES

SYLVIA'S HEROIN HOUSE

LUNCHEON DE DELIGHT

WINES

PALACES

CHAMPS ELYSÉES

WINE STORES

LE TOUR EIFFEL

RENOIR

PALACE

OPERA HOUSE

INVALIDES

CEZANNE

HASH

BUDDHA

MATISSE

APOLLO

OBELISQUE

MUSEUM D'ORSAY

DA VINCI

NOTRE

The LOUVRE

Michaelangelo

ILE DE LA CITÉ

POLICE STATION

St Michaels

DAME

MANET

PICASSO

VAN GOGH

SISLEY

BUSSTOP

GAUGUIN

MONET

SEURAT

LATIN QUARTER

RODIN

PISSARO

BIG + FOOD

KEROUAC

HEMINGWAY

SARTRE

LAUTREC

AUTRES

NOSTRADAMUS

ALOHA HOSTEL

LE PETIT JOURNAL

WINE

Paris

"Are you a Yankee fan or do you just like the cap?" I asked the kid in the otherwise empty train compartment. He just looked up toward the inside of the hat on his head and nodded.

"Do you speak any English?"

"You bet," he said enthusiastically. "I'm from Canada."

"Oh boy," I thought, "Here we go." I couldn't stand that expression "you bet." It was so perky. And why is everybody from Canada so fuckin' proud they're from Canada anyway? I mean what the hell is going on up there?

"Are these seats taken?" I asked.

"Nobody has been in to claim them as of yet," he replied. Didn't this guy just tell me he spoke English? 'Nobody has been in to claim them as of yet.' Give me a break – he was trying to save the compartment for himself.

"O.K. then," I said, moving in. "If you would kindly move your backpack from the seats that are adjacent to where you're sitting, I'll claim them, alright?"

My little buddy responded with a good old college try, hoisting his pack to the overhead luggage rack. I caught the metal frame on the way down towards my head. So much for my romantic illusions on board a train bound for Paris. I had just scoured the train looking for a compartment with Claudette Colbert's granddaughter waiting for me. No such luck and the train was filling up fast. Instead of winding away the miles with Ms. Napoleana, I might have to share the trip with ol' sparky here.

"I'm going to use the bathroom, could you please watch my big bag for me?"

Santana

"Well sure," he replied, "but you're not supposed to use the bathroom on the train while it is in the station."

"Gee, that's right." I went on, "I forgot, thanks. Let's hope you only let in a couple of thin women while I'm gone."

"Sure thing," he raved, "you can bet on it." Well there was some creativity – a little variation on the 'you bet' theme.

I made it through two and a half cars before I saw another candidate to share the ride. Through the compartment window our eyes met and her expression turned to one of the gravest concern. She looked away and went into deep intercessory prayer to the patron Saint of Anybody But Him. I opened the door and gave her a little "Boo," then walked on.

Another car and a half later, I had made my way to the front of the train where one of the porters was settling the account of a full compartment. They were closing the curtains as he checked off six little rectangles of green paper and put them in the slots provided next to the door on the outside of the compartment. I smiled, he smiled.

I asked, "the tickets are for?"

He said, "2 people, 2 tickets, 3 people, 3 tickets, 6 people," and motioned toward the door, "all full here." As he walked on to the next car, I pocketed four of the tickets he had just left. I hustled back to the love nest and found Junior alone reading his 40 lb. travel guide to Europe.

"The train is packed," I explained, "but I think we might be able to keep the compartment for ourselves. Have you got any cash on you, I'm fresh out." The kid wasn't that stupid. He dreaded the thought of the Simpsons sharing the ride as much as the next guy.

"All I have is this," as he held up ten Guilders.

"We've got to do this fast," I said as I took it. "I'll try to get change. Close the curtains, I'll be right back." I closed the door behind me, slipped the tickets in the slots and headed for the bar car.

The conductor made it to our compartment a good half an hour after the train had pulled out; "Only two?" he asked.

"Only two," I replied and he took our tickets without another word. Long after he was gone my new buddy was still waiting for me to say something.

"So are you a Yankee fan or what," I asked cordially.

The Drunken Tourist

"Well, sort of," was his response. I wondered how anyone could be sort of a Yankee fan. "I'm really a National League fan, but my main sport is hockey." Well, go figure. "How long have you been on the road?" he asked.

"Not long. How about yourself?"

"I left home eight months ago. I just flew into Amsterdam from Australia. Before that I was in Japan."

I was impressed. "You look in great shape for being on the road for eight months."

"I spent seven months in Japan on a residency to learn the language," he admitted.

"Like a student exchange deal then, right?"

"Yeah, sort of," he nodded.

"Did your family have to watch their kid?"

"No, it doesn't work like that," he said with an attitude. "I got sponsored by the investment banking firm I've been interning for. They paid for the trip mostly for me to learn Japanese."

I knew this kid was a budding yup. "Hey, that sounds fascinating," I replied sarcastically. "Would you mind if I took a look at that book of yours? There's a hostel in Paris that was recommended to me and I want to see if it's listed in there. Do you know Paris at all?"

"No, I've never been there. I did take three years of French in high school, though. I have an affinity for languages."

You can 'affinity' this, tough guy… "Where are you going to stay?" I asked instead.

"I made a reservation on line weeks ago at the Aloha Hostel. Good thing, too. You can bet the whole town is filled up this time of year."

Arghhh. This distinct possibility had been bugging me all day. And now I had to hear it from this kid?

"What's your name, anyway?"

"Jason. Jason Reilly."

"Oh, Lord," I exclaimed. "That's my ex-wife's name."

"Is she Irish?" he asked, all perked up.

"No," I said (of course she's Irish, you dope), "she used to be Irish, now she's Christian Science. Not that I have anything against Christian Science (I lied) it's just that she lost most of her personality in the process of the conversion."

"I never noticed that problem in our church," he said smoothly. "My father is a practitioner."

I felt like a dope. "Hey, I'm sorry, I didn't mean anything by it (I lied again). I just have a resentment going towards her and her cronies, that's all."

"It's all right, I'm used to it. Some things involved with our faith are hard to accept."

So there you go. We spent the better part of the train ride discussing how Mary Baker Eddie bakes spaghetti, the pros of faith healing and the cons of unnecessary bleeding. As I could best explain it, my problem with the Christian Science faith lay in the absence of any room for individual creativity, rather than in the basic precepts that are working in Science and Health. And where was Mr. Eddie, anyway? And why all those complicated little tabs for the correlative passages from the Bible? Even the Lord's Prayer wasn't open to inspirational interpretation anymore. Mary got all the fun jobs. Maybe Mr. Eddie was hard at work making the family fortune in the niche market of correlative tab manufacturing within the stationary supply business. No doubt, I contended, the practice of Christian Science could be a viable avenue toward the inevitable triumph of Spirit over "matter," but this avenue of theirs seemed all too exclusive, as if at the turn of the century, Mary & Company had cornered the market on salvation.

Jason adopted a pose on his dad's success. This exclusive avenue that I brought up, he explained, was the root to the degree of faith required for healing. This got me thinking. It was a fair point and he put it well. We were bonding a little, I suppose, so I dispensed with the diplomacy. "Last year my kid got his forehead semi-severely split open on the tennis court up at the Christian Science school. It wasn't deep, but he was gushing. He told me they went through a mummy's worth of gauze pads while they prayed like babies for half an hour before the bleeding stopped. Then they just band-aided him up. Now a couple of stitches from someone blessed with the God given craft of physicianship would have taken care of this easily. Instead, he's still walking around with a scar that he hates. Now why is a couple of stitches such a threat to these people's faith?"

"We would have called the doctor," Jason said calmly. "My dad only helps as the situation demands; we rely on God to do the rest."

The Drunken Tourist

"That sounds reasonable," I said, taking it easier. "Does your dad give credit to time as a factor in the healing process?"

"We concentrate on God as the only Truth. Truth doesn't recognize error," he stated firmly.

"Let me ask you something. When Mrs. Eddie defines all matter as error, why does this come across as a real insult to the Creator?"

"I don't know," he said. "Maybe the church's definition of matter isn't what yours is."

"Good answer," I said, and meant it. Jason succumbed to a smug smile. I snapped back, "it was the 'I don't know' part of your answer that I appreciated." Then I got to thinking how a religion that did not move forward by taking into consideration its own congregation's progressive contributions from "Divine Mind" is doomed, not to mention boring. The rewards of an alliance with the super-conscience is certainly not exclusive to Christian Science, anybody in Psychology 101 could tell you that. This exclusivity bothered me. Reliance for power from the source of all power is a given, isn't it? Go ask any drunk who's been to a couple of meetings.

Yet even if I didn't agree with all her teachings, Mrs. Eddie couldn't take the full rap for the present condition of her church. I didn't elaborate, for example, on how thin I thought their songs were, both in composition and delivery, or how nobody I ever met at their services had a recognizable sense of humor – how it always seemed like everybody was mostly concerned with acting "appropriate." All that was needed was to look at the current dynamic of any given congregation to rest the case. What were they up to? Were they a reasonably happy and loveable bunch? Was their acceptance of others sincere or just a patronizing tolerance? To these questions, two answers came to mind. The first was what I judged would come back to bite me. The second; how dead wrong I can be about whatever I want to be so damn right about.

* * *

The first thing I noticed when we arrived at the train station in Paris was the way America was represented – it was embarrassing. Billboards of terrible movies made in the U.S. of A. stood out like a fart in church. All these pictures of posers trying to look intense and comedians with their signature smiles. One picture of Billy Crystal and Robin Williams mugging it up for their current "tour de force" would end up following me around town like a stubborn piece of toilet paper trailing off my shoe.

The onslaught continued with McDonalds "Golden Arches." Golden showers are more like it. Maybe if I had ignored these little devils from the start they wouldn't have popped up every time I tried to capture a Monet-moment. Yet this yellow hue is shy compared to the pink of the 31 flavors, with uniforms to match. Maybe it wouldn't be so noticeable in a city other than Paris, but this shit really wasn't working. At the same time, I guess I should be grateful that Mr. Baskin and Mr. Robbins don't have the marketing clout that Nike has. Maybe fat check marks work through the cornfields of Nebraska, but in Paris? When I see that played out logo, I think of watching some knucklehead crying foul on a basketball court while this same joker is making ten million a year but still needs another ten million to put his name on a stinking tennis shoe. Why? Because he could 'just do it.' I mean, how much more money does this fella' have to have anyway? Or is it his competitiveness that drives him towards his sixth consecutive world title of 'the face you can't avoid?' At any rate, if I don't stay tuned, I may run the risk of our hero setting me straight on this problem I have about his money; communicating his explanation world wide via satellite through a cordless microphone at a televised celebrity dinner dance where he's the guest D.J., spinning his latest release after playing 18 holes of golf with a pool cue for his favorite charity that he's using as this year's tax write off.

Today, I'm joining the ranks of the snobby Parisians who can't stand all that crap. Today, a different pair of shoes for each day of the week could prove downright impractical, despite what the corporate golden boys might want me to think I deserve. Yeah, I know, "I'm worth it," but I'll have to find a way to carry on regardless. Just do it to someone else – I'm busy making my way through the Metro, only three stops away from the hostel where I can dump my luggage and hit the streets. My interpreter is right behind me, having more than a little trouble fitting his three story backpack through the turnstile. I figured Jason's adequate French and his 40 lb. travel guide might come in handy. Besides, I could trust him and if I didn't get a bed, Jason agreed he would stash my big bag with him for a day or two.

The Drunken Tourist

We arrived at the Aloha Hostel by midday, in time to pay but not in time to check in. The American kid at the desk had an attitude louder than the techno music he was blasting. Between two and five in the afternoon the rooms were closed, just like everything else in town. Our host made it clear how lucky I was to find a bed in the first place; so kiss some butt buddy or you're outahere.

Despite the lip from the clerk, the place looked promising. Two females came out of the kitchen area and one of them looked older than I was. The location turned out to be about a twenty minute walk from the Latin Quarter, which was fine except the hostel had a 2:00 a.m. curfew. At 2:05 the Gestapo sleeping behind the desk was not allowed to wake up no matter how hard you knocked on the door, which was situated about two meters from his head. Still, the lodging here was a welcome relief from the Amsterdam hatchery. It was six people max to a room, both male and female together. This came in handy at shower time. The girls shared their shampoo, conditioner and lotions liberally.

Before we caught our breath we met three girls from Australia. Reba, Dotty and Judy were sitting at one of the tables in the lobby writing postcards. They'd had a rough day of it already – getting lost while walking around town, trying to find a café they could afford on one of those romantic cobblestone streets, but ending up back in line at the one market that was open between 10:00 and 12:00, then again at 5:00 if you're lucky. This tale of woe deserved beers all around, and they were cheap enough, so I splurged, looking like the big spender for what amounted to about twelve dollars. From the start, it became abundantly clear that it was imperative to everyone that their experience in Paris be a memorable one. This sounded like a fine cause to me. We got the map out and spread it across the table, using our beers to hold it flat at the corners. The girls had been in town for three days and were having no fun at all. As the lowlight reels rolled, they reviewed the map for all the rotten luck they had along the way.

"Well, there's the Eiffel Tower," went Reba, " it's only a fifteen minute walk from here, but we waited in line for three hours in the brutal heat and got stuck in the elevator for ten minutes with a gang of Italian guys."

"Reba," Dotty said, "do you remember that awful aftershave? God, it was awful. Wasn't that aftershave awful, Reba?"

Santana

Jason was cracking up. I was interested in what the more subdued of the three had to say. "The walk down was fun," Judy stated, "you've got to admit the walk down was fun. It's worth the trip, ya know? How are you going to go home and not do the Eiffel Tower?"

"Well," answered Dotty, "How are we going to go home and not do the Louvre then?"

"The Louvre was closed." Reba looked at me, "the Louvre is closed on Monday." I figured these girls must have been out on the road for a while, having to repeat everything, but it turned out to be their style. Having to repeat everything had nothing to do with them being out on the road for a while, ya know?

Once they got through with their venting and had another beer, they were good company. I suggested they kiss up to the desk clerk and get him to put on some decent music with the volume down. They'd do it despite the fact that they hated the guy for hitting on every girl that checked in. They didn't give a shit if he heard them or not. It was good to get the update on the worldwide moratorium on hitting on two girls from the same group. Now we were confidants. They were going to freshen up and Jason was going on the internet. We would rendezvous for the sunset at the very end of the little island with the park between the bridges in the middle of the river. Then somebody came up with the brainstorm to check the map again for Ile de la Cité on the Seine. That would be the little island with the park between the bridges in the middle of the river, ya know? Meanwhile, I was headed for Le Tour D'Eiffel.

The girls were right. The line looked three hours long and it was sweltering out. Busloads of tourists were still coming. I took three different sets of snapshots of couples in the shadow of the Tower and still I was glad I had kept my Polaroid packed. Walking about hands free had already proven to make a world of difference. I felt less the foreigner. Even carrying my day bag wasn't half as liberating as walking with my hands and shoulders free and my pockets stuffed.

There was only one way to do the entry to the Tower: without hesitation. The old Van Gogh trick didn't work on the west entrance. Security was tight and the ticket takers must have surely heard a world of jive-osis in fifty languages by now. The guy that refused me entrance at the exit even watched as I strolled off into the crowd.

The Drunken Tourist

I reappeared at the east entrance area and approached the security guy to ask him to look clear across the way towards the other entrance to notice his co-worker looking for us to acknowledge him. I pointed all the way over there, and waved like I saw him and he saw me. "Look," I said, "you can see, yes?" There was no way the guy could positively identify what I was not looking at. I took out the snapshot of Alex while explaining in very broken English how he must be up ahead waiting for me with his Mom and all our stuff on the second level.

"There is this level, like over there, yes." I pointed up, then back again in the general direction of my previous attempt. I was confused. My wife was supposed to meet me at the elevator level on the west entrance. Knowing her, she was probably waiting right above us. Women, no sense of direction, ya know? I might have to walk all the way up the stairs. This was true. The poor fellow was frazzled enough to do the next logical thing; he did his own bit of waving to the next guy at the next check point ahead of him. Once he got his attention, he signaled to let me through. I walked the stairs to the mezzanine level and had to go through a similar negotiation with the elevator guy who demanded to see my ticket. At that point, however, it was almost a given that I must have had a ticket somewhere along the line, so he really didn't care that much. No doubt the suit and my lack of accoutrements played well. The pressing throngs didn't hurt my cause, either.

"This town I can do," I thought at the top. "It's all laid out right in front of me. I walk ovadare, thataway to the Arc thingamajig. Then from ovadare to overdare thataway down the Champs Street. From the Champs Street I can den go overdare overhere overdare to that little island with the park between the bridges in the middle of the river, ya know?" Transmitting towers must broadcast some kinda' slangwave through me or somethin'.

I carved my Diver tag on the wooden railing at the top of the viewing platform. I thought of my Queen one day leaning against this same spot and noticing it. Talk about obsessed – the girl was probably off with the nearest truck driver she could find, and I was in Paris still whining over her, over here. The Diver is a disassembled crucifix - Christ off the Cross. His arms are now outstretched in victory above his head. His body has the same pose that it would if it was still hanging on the cross, but with a little imagination it now looked like He might have a dignified dance going. His feet are supported by the cross that he used to be nailed to. If you get the picture from above, it looks like He has just spring-boarded into the beginnings of a swan dive. The Diver is diving into the depths of the divine, not hanging limp on a cross. I had one cast in silver with a ring for the chain on top of his head. Without any foresight on my part, the ring ended up looking like a halo. It's also a great tag; a quick and easy graffiti helping even the odds of the non-suffering Christ vs. the crucified one. The way I feel about it is almost the opposite of how I feel about all the "help me Jesus, I'm a useless sinner" songs and rhetoric. I figure my man would appreciate something depicting him that was a little more upbeat. I love Jesus and I know He loves me, even though I'm a useless sinner. I'm not afraid of creating something less than perfect. Lord knows I do it all day long anyway. He's just more accessible to my finite mind in the Diver pose than on a crucifix. That's all. When I find a better definition of Him, I'll move along with the higher power of it.

Across the bridge at the foot of the Tower, I made my way to L'Arc de Triomphe. The traffic somehow circling the structure was mesmerizing. God was certainly at work here. I had a nectarine and a roll leaning up against the Arc and then snoozed off. An hour later, I was rudely awakened by a policeman. How lovely it was to then discover two huge wads of bird shit half baked into my suit.

Who wouldn't feel like an emperor walking down Les Champs Élysees? It felt simply grand. Fuck the McDonald's, I was walking straight ahead to the Obelisque on the horizon. The consumer crowd could have their harried shopping all to themselves. Even the traffic would have to wait for this procession of one to reach the bull's eye. I was straight on the mark toward the center of the circle, all dumbstruck with how stupendous the whole layout was. They couldn't have made this up as they went along, or could they? What a massive undertaking even one statue must have been. Did they know how good it would look before they hoisted it up there? And if it didn't work out, were the contractors' heads chopped off?

The Drunken Tourist

Probably not; if so, there would have been a statue of a pile of heads somewhere. The current tenants of these spectacular buildings surrounding me had to be the descendents of the Good King LifeasArt and his steady Queen ArtasLife who, a couple of hundred years ago, orchestrated this whole creative explosion as a testimony to the rest of the universe of what a marvelous species we are.

Up ahead there was a crowd sunning themselves around the shallow pool in the park before the Louvre. I took a seat and waited for the fountain in the center to do its thing. I expected it would erupt in some kind of sublime aquatic ballet at any minute but nothing happened. What a party pooper. I don't know how everybody sitting around could just let this little pisser relieve itself in the middle of all this splendor. It must have been on the fritz or something. My king surely wouldn't have tolerated this pee-pee going on with Apollo in the neighborhood, that's for sure.

The two fountains directly outside the museum were more like it. Most people had their shoes off and pant legs rolled up, kicking the water around to join in the splash dance. The rhythms of the water held my attention for a good half hour. I liked the last splurges at the top especially. It was as if these diehard spurts were consciously sacrificing themselves only after they knew they had reached the top to crown the whole package, unaware that their life was not over, but eternal in the nature of the mechanism itself. I wondered if these last gaspers might eventually recognize that they too were naturally eternal and start to enjoy the ride – realizing way before their turn at the top that there was a lot of fun going on supporting their buddies in the base and the body of the fountain.

* * *

A conga player was playing his little rhythm along with the Seine when I arrived for my rendezvous with Jason and the girls on the Ile de la Cité. I was early, armed with two cheap bottles of French red wine, prepared to salute the sunset in fine fashion. The hunt for a reasonable liquor store had taken me north of the Louvre to the fringes of the Montmarte district. It was my first glimpse of the Paris I remembered from the old musicals I used to watch. The streets were fairly well closed up for the holidays, much like New York in August, but I didn't care. One good Leslie Caron and a little rain would more than make up for all the absent locals that could afford to get out of town this time of year.

The first bottle of red was already half gone by the time the fellow hitting those drums took a break. I offered him a taste and hoped he'd stop for a while but he declined on both counts.

"What kind of wine do you have there, Monsieur?" I heard from my left bank.

"It's red," I said coldly as I turned to see this young Frenchman sitting next to me with a guitar case at his side.

"Well," he said, "I prefer Rosé, but you seem like a nice fellow, so I will try some of your wine."

This was too audacious to brush off. "You mean you could do me this favor then, yes?" I said, all thick with New York.

"Yes, yes," he continued, picking right up on my sarcasm, "after I try some, I will even let you know if it is worth your finishing."

"Well, that is very big of you," I replied, "pity we have no stemware handy."

"No matter, I will suffer through," he said with a smile and I handed him the bottle. You've got to respect a guy with this kind of nerve.

Daniel was a native on the prowl. Educated in both English and French from his first years in school, these days he mostly played guitar by the river and hit on foreign girls on holiday. His repertoire consisted of 60's and 70's classics that weren't the usual, played-out numbers you might hear in any public park from Venice Beach to Washington Square.

Hendrix's "Little Wing" captured the mood beautifully and a nice rendition of Paul Simon's "Diamonds on the Soles of her Shoes" worked well with steady-eddie over there on the congas. The sky was changing on cue and the water followed suit. After our little set, I watched Daniel's guitar while he made a quick run across the bridge to the north side of the Seine to buy us a nice little slab of black hash which cost me about ten bucks. I could see him negotiating on the other side of the river with a group hanging out on the far bank along the water. In less than a minute's time he broke from the huddle and waved back happily across the way, returning with that walk that spells score.

The Drunken Tourist

We had quite the merry crew together once Jason and the girls showed up. The sunset was such a dramatic winner that even the conga player held still for a while. The girls were loving it, making sure this evening would be on their highlight reels, but Jason seemed to remain a bit too collected even for him. Just by the look on his face you could tell he was homesick. Sweet twilights on the Seine can do that to a guy. In between all the wonderful verses I heard those sad refrains myself. Why would anybody not want to share their greatest hits with the ones they love?

I told the entourage I was off to get another bottle of wine and on the way out caught up with Jason wandering off on his own. "Could you walk with me to the store for a minute?" I asked.

"Well sure, I'll take the walk," he replied.

"Thanks," I said. "I could use the company." We carried on without a word until we reached the top of the stairs and headed north on the bridge. Towards the end of the expanse, I changed my walk dramatically. My feet hit the ground with my step a tad duckish, while my arms swung loose and wider than usual. My posture straightened up automatically. I took the first turn sharp, yet considerate, as I continued to concentrate on keeping my feet turned out for a more open stance than I naturally had.

"What on earth are you up to?" laughed Jason.

"This is how my Queen walks," I explained, "when she gets a good rhythm going her walk is invincible. And believe it or not, it's very sexy."

It felt better to be in her shoes than to think of her not being here. Now I could see a bit of what she might favor along the way with more certainty. "You see that restaurant up ahead," I said, "she would try to use the bathroom just to see if it measured up to the rest of the splendid décor they've got going."

"She sounds like a trip," Jason said, perking up a bit.

"She's a trip all right," I went on. "Did you ever spend ten hours straight with someone and figure out it was only two hours later?"

"Yeah sure," whispered Jason, "like long summer days at home."

That got me. "She was my summer at home," I said, finding myself again making my own way down the street.

Santana

Supplies in hand, I tried my kid on the way back. His walk was less studied of course, with some footwork that would give Gene Kelley pause to consider. First a little Bebop, then a good grunge prance, throw in some Michael Jackson without the affectations, a Bruce Lee bounce and there you have it. He could anticipate the breaks in the masses trudging along and use them as walking rhythms by the age of ten. Parking meters, vendors, and slowpokes were welcome obstacles for a little drum roll action in his stride. At corners waiting for the light to turn he would keep one knee jerking or foot tapping so not to break his tempo. The hands would be working, too. Open palmed, then rubbing together, occasionally hitting the air without the corny, conspicuous flash. "This is my boy!" I shouted as I hopped around on the way. "What can I say, the kid's a star." Jason was back, and I was O.K. as we rejoined the crew on the Ile de la Cité.

Quite the crowd had surrounding the girls by the time we got back. There was no way I was breaking out my bottle in the midst of all this – I was on the verge of a good drunk. "Daniel," I asked, "Do you know any decent bars around where we might find a piano?"

"My friend," he said, "I didn't know you played. This is good news. Why don't we try this spot that I know. It's not far from here, but it may well be closed for the holidays."

"Do you think there might be a few women there?"

"There usually are. Besides, we have your friends with us. What is that blonde's name again, please?"

"Her name is Dotty, but I really don't think you have a shot. Just make sure you have settled on her before you piss off all three of them, O.K.? Maybe let her come to you for a change, because once she turns you down, that's it, O.K.?"

"Yes, yes, I understand," he said. "How do you say, they are good people?"

"Yes, that's right, that's how we say it. They are good people."

By the time I started really jonesing for some hard liquor, our entourage was off to Daniel's bar. It was very different to walk in a party of six, compared to two, much less the party of one I was used to. I didn't like the pressure; having to take into consideration everyone's

The Drunken Tourist

moves and preferences. It was good Daniel was leading. I had already found that asking directions in this city was pretty much a waste of time. If someone did have the inclination to help out, the route that they would recommend would usually be too complicated. One wrong turn and there went all those beautiful plans. Then again, if I asked someone for a spot or a street name that they might be somewhat familiar with, they would stop to contemplate the question long enough to let me know that they really weren't sure which way was the best way to go. Then I would be obligated to try their suspect route. Half the time what I was looking for was right around the corner, anyway. At least New Yorkers make it clear either way without even breaking stride.

Daniel's bar was closed as predicted. Now the group was confronted with one of those awkward social moments; loitering around outside a boarded up restaurant on the outskirts of the Latin Quarter and not wanting to admit our options were severely limited. Nobody had any real money to spend and everybody wanted to keep partying. Daniel suggested another bar that was a few metro stops away but the prevailing mood seemed to say stay on the streets. Instead of collectively managing a big night at a cool bar in Paris, we paired off, then switched places, paused when somebody wanted to pause, took turns trying to sound inspired over some nonsense that looked interesting, laughed it off, had more wine, made fun of other clueless wanderers on holiday who were doing the same thing, smoked more hash and basically created general havoc and revelry along our way. It was 1:30 by the time we all stumbled back to the doors of the hostel. We carried on inside until they kicked us out of the lobby at 3:00. Dotty kept the clerk busy long enough for us to smuggle Daniel upstairs to crash in an empty bunk in their room. Who knows what happened from there.

Rather than wait for the verdict the next morning, I hit the Louvre first thing. Completely overwhelmed by the monstrosity of the whole layout, I sat down in the first vacant seat I found in one of the third floor Renaissance hallways.

Like a Puerto Rican in Harlem, a young lady sashayed her way past me three times before I waved her down. There was no way there was a museum tape coming through her headphones with that stroll she had working.

Santana

"Excuse me, miss," I mouthed my hello with my right forefinger pointed John the Baptist style. "I would love to know what you're listening to," came out a little loud for the room as she necked her headphones.

"It's an Italian hip-hop band I'm sure you never heard of," she replied in good English.

"Well, you've got the right country for the room we're in."

"Well, I guess you're right," she replied, "but the Italians own the whole place anyway, don't you think?"

"It's too early to tell," I answered. "I just got here. Did you notice how everyone's always pointing in all these paintings?"

"Pointing where?"

"I don't know. Just pointing, usually up to the heavens, I guess. Could we walk together for a while? You'll see what I mean. I'd like to get back to John the Baptist; he's got the best point going I've seen so far."

"It is the light from that painting that makes it the masterpiece it is, not his finger, for Christ's sake," she answered. "Come, I will show you what to look for."

Sylvia from Bologna knew her art all right. She was writing her thesis on some style of fresco work done in Northern Italy during the time of Michelangelo. She was also a bit of a junkie. You could see it on her face in the sun when we found a table on the balcony of the museum café. From there I guess she felt it was a good time to confess a little to an interested stranger she'd probably never see again. The carafe of white wine she was drinking may have helped.

I was going with gin today, bought a few blocks away before coming in. Her current bender had started innocently enough and now her hours were numbered before she was headed back to Italy, unprepared to start her next semester. I sympathized as best I could, although I sort of have a rule never to talk about not drinking and drugging when I'm drinking and drugging.

When I finally got a word in, I mentioned I was on the hunt for a bed that I could rent for the week so I could comfortably afford to stay in Paris. She immediately suggested her friend's place where she had been staying.

Past my fountain and the Opera House, we stopped at the store

The Drunken Tourist

for more wine and a pack of cigarettes. Another fourteen blocks later we were at her buddy's apartment. And what a fucking dump it was.

The whole place smelled like cat piss. Old newspapers everywhere with empty bottles and dirty dishes on all available table space. Sylvia didn't even apologize as she cleared a path to the kitchen. The cat litter box was stationed on the floor next to the refrigerator.

Sylvia rolled a joint while I opened the wine at the counter. I figured her buddy wasn't home, but then again we could have missed him on the way into the kitchen. Halfway through the joint she laid out a couple of lines of dirt. "Would you like a snort?" she asked.

"If it's Heroin," I replied. "I could only stand a little."

"It is very pure," she replied. "You will have no trouble with this, even if you are not used to it."

"All right then, I'll just do a little line."

Within ten minutes the apartment didn't look that bad after all. After fifteen, I stopped kicking the cat that kept rubbing itself on my pants. "Ahh yes," I thought, "everything is in order. It's nice to relax for a change. The tile on this floor is so lovely."

Sylvia was in the other room packing. "Hey Sylvia, where's the ashtray?" I yelled out.

"Go ahead and help yourself," she responded.

"No, no. Where's the ashhhhtray?

"No really, it's alright."

" I think I'm good. Really. I just need an ashtray."

"Madonna Mia! If I say it's alright, it's alright!"

"Fuck it," I thought, "Why not? The litter box is in flicking distance anyway." By the time I finished my cigarette I was in the bathroom puking my guts out. In between heaves, I noticed the tile in the bathroom was much nicer than in the kitchen.

"Sylvia, I've got to go," I announced.

"Don't you want to wait for Pierre to get home?" she shouted back.

"No, that's all right, I have an appointment to get to."

"Wait a moment, I will write down my cell phone number in Bologna for you. When you get to Italy you can look me up."

"All right then." She came out of the bedroom in her underwear with a scrap of paper in her hand.

"Here you are, my sweet. I will be settled in next week. Please call and I will show you around Bologna. It is a marvelous city."

Santana

We kissed cheek to cheek then she planted a sloppy one on the lips that sobered me up long enough to head for the door in earnest. I left her a sandwich from the Louvre to remember me by.

It was dark out when I woke up in the back of a van with a grill on the back door window. I had no shoes or socks on and my pants were damp up to my knees. Blackout panic hit me as I checked my pockets. Fuck. Nothing. No identification or money. Fuck. I had to be in custody. I prayed I was in custody. This had to be a police van.

It was almost a relief to be herded into the station house.

"Monsieur Santana, is it, yes?" I was asked by a second policeman behind the processing desk.

"Yes, that's me. Do you have my identification?"

"Oui, your identification is here, along with the rest of your belongings. You are a tourist here in Paris, yes?"

"Yes sir, I apologize for my condition sir, but.."

He cut me off. "Sit down over there and just answer the questions."

"Yes sir." I was shitting. He was filling out a fair amount of paperwork.

"Monsieur Santana," he stated. "You are being ticketed for public intoxication and unlawful trespass. If you cannot pay the fine, you will stay here until you see the magistrate on Monday." I prayed I heard him right. What the hell happened, anyway?

"Thank you sir," I said. "I sincerely apologize for what happened. I last remember walking down the street feeling very sick." A collective laugh ensued. From what I could understand, I must have had a little play day in one of their fountains somewhere in the district. They had found me passed out in a chair I had moved into the pool that surrounded the fountain. Thank God I had enough money on me. I paid the fine, signed the papers, gave them the address of the hostel, and got the hell out of there. God, was I lucky. If this was L.A., I would be going through processing in County Jail right now. What was I thinking? Gin and Heroin don't mix. Man, was I stupid. My trip could have ended right there.

I hugged the Seine looking for landmarks on the way back to the Latin Quarter. From across the Palace bridge I saw him. Could it be? Sure enough, it was St. Michael slaying the Dragon.

The Drunken Tourist

The power of the statue hit me hard. I kneeled down at the base and said my prayers of guilt. One good stake through the throat could do it. "Go ahead, Michael," I prayed. "I'm all yours, change me." This sounded truly ridiculous, even to myself. Who knows how sad it may have sounded to anybody else that might be listening. I knew better than this – my part had to be done. If everybody in the world that prayed for deliverance had been granted their wish, what good would it do anyway? We would all end up being more ungrateful and lazy than we are now. That still small voice inside then whispered, "start applying what you might say to other people to yourself or shut up."

Sleep was in order and tomorrow was Sunday. I had promised Urantia Book readings in the park to the crew at the hostel.

* * *

I found a disillusioned group waiting for me at breakfast. They were left hanging last night and apparently my no-show had brought them closer together. Here was that sympathy bond again – comaraderie in the face of a common evil. Only this time, I was that face.

"I apologize for last night," I stated sincerely, "I got loaded and ended up getting arrested."

"We figured as much," Jason said coldly as he got up from the table. The girls were a little more tolerant but still you could sense that our spell had been broken.

"After breakfast, could we still read in the park as planned?" I pleaded.

Dotty spoke up, "We'll go for a while, but then we have plans. Jason is taking us to the Louvre at noon."

"The line might be ridiculous on Sunday at noon," I said. "Would you consider a little bus tour instead?"

"Well, I don't know," she answered. "We'll see how it goes."

We gathered together in the little park around the corner from the hostel shortly after breakfast. I suggested we take turns reading. Dotty started by arbitrarily opening the book to an earmarked page 1475:

"To the traveler from Britain he said, 'My brother, I perceive you are seeking for truth, and I suggest that the spirit of the Father of all truth may chance to dwell within you.

Did you ever sincerely endeavor to talk with the spirit of your own soul? Such a thing is indeed difficult and seldom yields consciousness of success; but every honest attempt of the material mind to communicate with its indwelling spirit meets with certain success, notwithstanding the majority of all such magnificent human experiences must long remain as superconsciousness registrations in the souls of such God-knowing mortals."

Dotty paused while everyone looked around at each other without saying a word. Then she continued:

"To the runaway lad Jesus said: 'Remember, there are two things you cannot run away from – God and yourself. Wherever you may go, you take with you yourself and the spirit of the heavenly Father which lives within your heart. My son, stop trying to deceive yourself; settle down to the courageous practice of facing the facts of life; lay firm hold on the assurances of sonship with God and the certainty of eternal life, as I have instructed you. From this day on purpose to be a real man, a man determined to face life bravely and intelligently."

What a charge. She continued:

"To the condemned criminal he said at the last hour: 'My brother, you have fallen on evil times. You lost your way; you became entangled in the meshes of crime. From talking to you, I well know you did not plan to do the thing which is about to cost you your temporal life. But you did do this evil, and your fellows have adjudged you guilty; they have determined that you shall die. You or I may not deny the state this right of self-defense in the manner of its own choosing. There seems to be no way of humanly escaping the penalty of your wrongdoing. Your fellows must judge you by what you did, but there is a Judge to whom you may appeal forgiveness, and who will judge you by your real motives and better intentions. You need not fear to meet

the judgment of God if your repentance is genuine and your faith sincere. The fact that your error carries with it the death penalty imposed by man does not prejudice the chance of your soul to obtain justice and enjoy mercy before the heavenly courts."

"Wow," exclaimed Jason, the first to speak up. "That was really Jesus saying that?"

"It doesn't even matter that much who it was," exclaimed Dotty, "I got the chills reading it."

"I know how you feel," I replied. "I don't know how much clearer I need to be shown. My spirit always responds to this and I keep spitting on all my blessings."

"Heavenly Father Mother God," Jason interjected, "thank you for all our blessings and keep us faithful to a clean heart. Teach us to be satisfied in the truth and beauty of your Kingdom. We need not look any further than to you for all our desires…" He kept going for a while. We were locked in, astounded by his eloquence and power, faithful to the moment.

After a good bit of silence, Reba volunteered to read on. She opened to page 578 and read from The Local Universe, Paper 50, #7. entitled:The Rewards of Isolation, presented by a Secondary Lanonandek Son of the Reserve Corps:

"On first thought it might appear that Urantia and its associated isolated worlds are most unfortunate in being deprived of the beneficent presence and influence of such superhuman personalities as a Planetary Prince and a Material Son and Daughter. But isolation of these spheres affords their races a unique opportunity for the exercise of faith and for the development of a peculiar quality of confidence in cosmic reliability which is not dependent on sight or any other material consideration. It may turn out, eventually, that mortal creatures hailing from the worlds quarantined in consequence of rebellion are extremely fortunate. We have discovered that such ascenders are very early intrusted with numerous special assign-

ments to cosmic undertakings where unquestioned faith and sublime confidence are essential to achievement."

"On Jerusem the ascenders from these isolated worlds occupy a residential sector by themselves and are known as the agondonters, meaning evolutionary will creatures who can believe without seeing, persevere when isolated, and triumph over insuperable difficulties even when alone. This functional grouping of the agondonters persists throughout the ascension of the local universe and the traversal of the superuniverse; it disappears during the sojourn in Havona but promptly reappears upon the attainment of Paradise and definitely persist in the Corps of the Mortal Finality. Tabamantia is an agondonter of finaliter status, having survived from one of the quarantined spheres involved in the first rebellion ever to take place in the universe of time and space. All throughout the Paradise career, reward follows effort as a result of causes. Such rewards set off the individual from the average, provide a differential of creature experience, and contribute to the versatility of ultimate performances in the collective body of the finaliters."

"So we are agondonters then?" asked Dotty.

"Among other things, yes," I said.

"It all sounds so out there," she continued. "Will we recognize each other then?"

"Apparently so. I'll be looking forward to see what you look like in a couple of thousand years."

"Where does it say a couple of thousand years?"

"I don't remember, but there's a lot of space out there. It could take a while."

We all laid back and soaked in the sun for a while before we headed back to the hostel to continue our day. The girls were off to the Louvre with Jason and I was going to hop on one of those convertible buses to see the sights from a fresh perspective. The next few days in Paris were to be consciously dedicated to renew my mind, body, and soul through the mass consumption of good books and fine

The Drunken Tourist

art. I convinced myself that the genius of the masters could obliterate all gross fermentations and become my cure.

From the west corner of Notre Dame Esplanade, I hopped through the rear exit door of the tour bus, up the spiral stairs to the open-air level on top. I sank into my choice of ten or twelve empty seats that were radiating the blaring sun. From this height the gargoyles perched against the church were almost within reach. I suppose they were designed to look menacing, but they seemed quite unaffected to me – almost bored. Like a security guard at a nursing home working the graveyard shift who was memorizing Shakespeare on the job. A closer look disclosed these guys had real personality. Not your average one dimensional evil demons on the loose. Being stuck on a church for 500 years could make anyone a little docile.

I stayed on the bus for two full tours. Around most every corner came a new piece of craftsmanship to admire. Even if it didn't knock me out I had to admire the work involved. Past the Rodin Museum, to the Palace des Invalids, the Eiffel Tower, down the Champs to the Louvre, past the Museum D'Orsay, back through the Latin Quarter and round again. My bladder held out long enough to make it back to the entrance of the Museum D'Orsay. The Louvre had already kicked my ass with its monstrous layout and centuries of artwork proving much too intimidating for my frail sense of art appreciation. Once lost in that labyrinth, the best I could do was count missing body parts of ancient Romans and Greek tragedies. I wasn't going to let any of that happen here. The Museum D'Orsay was supposed to be a temple of proven impossibilities – work done that could not be done – divine spit in the eye of protocol. The prospect of not identifying with at least a portion of the work was a real threat to my own sense of creativity. It seemed imperative that I relate on some significant level.

A perusal around the building itself was the first order of business. Here was a magnificent train station renovated at the turn of the century into the transportation center it is today. At the entrance of the Museum Gift Shop, I discovered the first breach in the security net towards free passage into the land that time could not forget.

Looking through the glass double doors you could see to the far end of the portico to what looked like the bookstore exit and subsequent entrance to the ground floor of the museum. Before entering, I reached into my day bag and grabbed my faithful novel to prominently display Magister Ludi in my left hand. Then, with an attitude of habitual conformity exuding from mind and body, I walked through the store checkout sensors, past the security guards and into a pantheon of marble and iron, plaster and stone. It seemed my little Glass Bead Game had worked, as Mercie's "David" welcomed me into the inner sanctuary of the temple.

How did these sculptors ever pull this off? Forget first impressions for a second, what about the sheer labor involved? What happened if they made a mistake? Did they have to start all over again, or did they go with the flow and eventually change the original vision just a tad? I'm sure they planned it out beforehand, but there still must have been some very delicate moments along the way. All I knew was that I had to sit down. Nobody here was getting lucky – these guys were serious. The best response I could come up with was a simple and silent surrender to the genius surrounding me.

As if on cue from my newly adopted attitude of acceptance, there was old St. Michael himself, this time in a suit of battered bronze. The guy was on my tail all right. No way to shake him.

What I wouldn't have done right there and then for a few good bangs into that armor of his. After all, we had been hounding each other even since I bought a Pic N' Save picture of him and his animal for 99 cents years ago. It always stayed leaning against the bathroom window so you could see the sunlight shine in through the flimsy matting from the back of the frame while relieving yourself. Today, however, my man motivated me directly to the top floor of the masters.

The other museum patrons disappeared as the water and sky of Sisly and Monet ushered me in to the scenes of Manet and Toulouse-Lautrec, working the halls like local barflies. You couldn't ask for a better group of hosts for a party. Even the cafeteria turned out to be more hospitable than expected. Besides the usual "Sandwich con Gratis," an excellent red wine was available in a convenient to-go size.

I must have gone in and out of those top floor rooms twenty times in the next few days, saluting Lautrec's characters with my bottles of red and toasting Gaugin with Tequila. Day two found me all sappy for Van Gogh on rum and hash while Cezanne and Pis-

The Drunken Tourist

sarro would diligently stabilize my moods as my soul danced 'round the neighborhood.

Matisse's "Luxury, Calm and Delight" pretty much entitled my time, but if I had to pick a singular favorite it would have to be Redon's "Buddha." When I knew it was time to go for good, I sucked this baby up one last time and held it in the breath of my mind's eye until long after I was out the double doors and back walking the streets with the D'Orsay hoodlums now in tow.

* * *

Daniel and I, the girls and Jason all shared one more good twilight together before I was headed for Barcelona.

In between The River Seine's Greatest Hits I even got a chance to rework my old standard "Cure for the Blues" on the guitar. It's one of those numbers that you can easily change the lyric around with a good mistake or two and still end up getting lucky. This evening the words worked out as follows:

> *Here I was thinking...*
> *someone actually was loving me*
> *Once again I'm dreaming...all in black and white*
> *'cause I woke to the colors of...*
> *A crooked heart...in a haunted house*
> *That seems to burn, burn everything*
> *Just because it can...*
> *Still I got The Cure for the Blues*
> *I'll refuse to entertain even a little bit of it*
> *It's so far beyond me I'm crashin' and spinnin'...*
> *All the way back to the land of the living.*

So it wasn't perfect. Nobody cared. We were jamming; quite content to relish in present company. It was more than good enough for the time being, which was somehow good enough for me. This would be plenty for our highlight reels. We all had that sense that it could be a couple of thousand years before we might see each other again.

TO LA MANCHA
ESTA BIEN!
BARCELONA
VIENNA
RHUMBA!
CERVANTES
LAS RAMBLAS
SAMBA!
GAUDI
BAD DRUNK
FIESTA!
BEAUTIFUL HIGH
COLUMBUS
GABRIEL'S POW WOW
PALMA
CHOPIN
NOW!
MALLORCA

Barcelona & Mallorca

While I waited at the Gare de Leon for the night train to southern France, somebody recommended purchasing a sleeper car supplement to my Europass for this leg of the trip. The extra dollars proved to be well spent. On the supplement there is a space at the bottom that you are supposed to fill out with the date of the day you are traveling. The conductor then stamps over the date you entered and takes his copy. All went according to plan, except when my conductor took the supplement he forgot to stamp my Europass. This turned out to be a real piece of luck. Now I had an extra day on my pass.

After the best night's sleep I had in about two months, I woke up twenty minutes outside the last stop in France where you transfer trains to go on to Barcelona. On the platform I spotted two women with a young child waiting for our train. I asked them to watch my big bag while I ran up the stairs to mail some postcards. By the time I returned, three or four minutes before the train was scheduled to pull out, my bag was sitting alone. Once I boarded and settled in, I searched the train, ready to scold the culprits who had abandoned my bag. That's when I got my first good look at Melissa. She smiled and apologized for not waiting on the platform for a minute longer and I smiled and apologized for not being there a minute earlier. Within the space of three sentences I was on my knees in the aisle, proposing coffee in the bar car.

The train trip that I had envisioned between Amsterdam and Paris was now coming true as we hugged the Mediterranean coastline, seated at the window of an otherwise empty bar car. The train would turn a corner and reveal a view of dazzling beaches at the base of jagged cliffs with sailboats bobbing in emerald waters a swimmer's distance from shore. Even Melissa herself kept getting better looking, way before we switched to beer after breakfast. She had that type of deep good looks you usually miss when you're on the prowl. Traveling alone on her summer break from the University of California at Santa Cruz, she had just spent the last week in Rome and didn't even bore me much with how rude the Italian men were. She was too involved with the beauty of our present position to care for all that.

At one point she looked straight at me and said, "Isn't this just wonderful?" Yes it was. It really couldn't have been any finer. We noticed the same things at the same time. We got along with our fellow travelers like we had been together for years. We drank at the same pace and agreed to dispense with the past in honor of the finest ride the world had to offer. I was usually the one that went too far, too fast, but now Melissa was happily taking the lead to make the most of the moments. This all transferred to a sense of harmony with the opposite sex that I had almost forgotten. We knew we were going to have a marvelous time together in Barcelona without even talking about it. It was already happening.

The only plan we made was that we would first go to the hotel where she had made a reservation. It was on the Avinguda de Roma, a stone's throw from the train station. If need be, I could wait until tomorrow to investigate the hostel that was recommended by Jonathan back on the train to Berlin. Fifteen minutes before the train was to pull into Barcelona, our bartender closed the bar with a round for us on him. I paid the tab for the drinks and Melissa got the tip. We had already split the breakfast bill years ago. We agreed to meet on the platform after we got our things together and exited the train.

The train pulled in and I walked down the platform a few cars' length to where I estimated Melissa would get off. I waited until the crowd thinned and the train pulled out of the station before I started to panic. Where the hell was she? Did she fall asleep on the train, or had I missed her on the platform while she went upstairs to exit? I burned up the stairs, my big bag slapping behind me. No sign of her. Up another staircase to the elevator, still no sign of her.

The Drunken Tourist

I combed the streets in every direction: nothing. I hurried back down the escalator, looked around, then down the staircases back to the platform. She had to be waiting for me at the end of the platform, in the fog of the train exhaust with a raincoat on and a fedora. Still nothing. All the way back to the street level in a sweat and still no Melissa.

There was no way she ditched me. Or did she? No way, I wasn't even that drunk. I looked for Avinguda de Roma on the corners and then asked someone where it was. All I heard was that it was far. Liar. I asked again. Same answer. Shit. There are two train station stops in Barcelona, you fucking knucklehead. I had jumped the fucking gun again. "Taxi! Avinguda de Roma at the train station."

How do you say 'Hurry' in Spanish? "Let me off here," I demanded as we pulled up near Saints Station. Then the cab driver had the nerve to ask for money. I paid the guy his freakin' fare, then went in the station to find the platform our train must have pulled in to. It was long gone. After ten minutes of spinning around the station, I found a counter bar and ordered whatever. I kept scanning the crowds, wasting my time. Aviguda de Roma was waiting.

"Hola, do you speak English?" I asked the concierge at the Expo Hotel right outside the station.

"Yes sir, what can I do for you?"

"I'm looking for an American girl that must have just checked in. Her name is Melissa – brown hair about this long, carrying a backpack – beautiful girl; have you seen her?"

"Do you have a last name, sir?"

"No," I said impatiently. "Could you pull up your reservations for today, please?" Nothing. "Anything with the first initial M?" Still nothing. "How many hotels along the Avenue here?"

"There is the Abbott and the Hotel Roma as you walk toward Ciudat Vella."

"Muchos gracias," I replied and hurried out. The Hotel Roma had to be it.

Of course she wasn't there and of course I was cursed.

Big bag in tow, I walked back to the station, down to the red line, transferred to the blue line and eventually made it to the hostel where I had planned to stay.

Santana

It was very civilized, with a balcony and kitchen and living room
with four men to a room. "Well isn't this just splendid," I thought,
"Melissa would have really liked this place." Turns out the hostel
curfew was 1:00 A.M. and Barcelona wakes up at about midnight.
I showered and changed and figured I'd be back sometime around
seven in the morning.

The Festival of the Virgin Mary's Second Cousin's Half-Sister's
Landlord was in full swing by the time I surfaced in the middle of
the Old City. Any excuse for a party would do. The streets here
were everything I imagined the streets of Paris would be. Sharp
turns on cobblestones, no cars, laundry stretched window to
window, two and three floors up. And the music! The Samba got
a hold of my legs and didn't let go. The Rumba didn't hurt a bit
either. There were bands playing to the crowds in the squares where
everyone was drinking and dancing around together. I mean really
together. Arm in arm, cheek to cheek, hip to hip, dips and spins
like it was nothing. It was all so engrossing, I only looked for my
Melissa every other minute. There were stand-up bars on almost
every corner and everyone was "Hola, Hola." I got drunker than
hell, but my legs kept going. These legs that I had thought were
mine had been living on a steady diet of the down beat for so long
that now that they were getting their over-due of the off beat, they
had an agenda all their own. They were buckling on cue. So that's
how they do it. Yeah, I got it. Get over here, senorita. Let me take
you for a little spin. Go ahead, now you spin me; go ahead, I'm new
here... you take the lead. Closer now, ouch! Sorry, sorry – oh yeah,
there ya go, spin me one more time – now double-spin me. Watch
this one; you ready? OK, here we go... You like that? No? Sorry...
Drink? No? O.K., bye bye. NEXT... "Hola, por favor? A little slower this time, please. Oh yes, that's sweet... now I'm suave, stay with
me now, I'm just getting this. Estabien, Estabien! Gracias! Drink?
No? O.K., Adios!" These folks knew what time it was alright. The
last I remembered it was after four.

I woke up in broad daylight with my back against a pile of sheetrock.
It was leaning up against the wall of a building right on the sidewalk.
The good citizens of the old city must have been stepping around me

The Drunken Tourist

for hours. My precious day bag was sitting right there next to me and my blue suit was filthy with dust. The rebel legs were stilting on me now and my head had that groove still beating. Otherwise, I was in fine shape. I really liked this town. All that was missing was Melissa and perhaps a good, strong, wake-up drink to get the old psychic antennae up to finding her.

This place was L.A. deluxe. People were actually saying hello and walking at the same time. Imagine that. Everybody looked you in the eye. Go figure. The 1.5 Second Rule must have had its origins here. They even had a beach with water that you could swim in. I stripped down to my boxers and dove right in to bury at sea the old, hungover man that I had expected to live with for the day. Five minutes later, I reappeared on shore, all miraculously tan and toned. Yeah right. Still, I knew it was only a matter of time before one of these topless bathing beauties would flag down the skinny, white-assed and red faced American sitting there in the sand with his dusty blue suit laid out for a dry cleaning.

After ten or fifteen minutes I figured they'd have to wait till to-night on the dance floor to get a hold of me. I was off to find a little shade. Along the walk that ribboned the beach, across the fold-out bridge, and past the Monument of Columbus, I found the refuge I was looking for on Las Ramblas. Plenty of shade, plenty of people, no vehicles and no charge to sit down along the way. I bought a pocket bottle of rum and splurged on a Coke so I could sit at a table, strike a few poses, and suck it all in. Any minute now Melissa would come strolling down the promenade in her Catalan Blue summer dress, searching for me.

My legs got drunk again in no time and took off on me into the heart of the city. We found ourselves at the Barcelona Cathedral. These Spaniards had it going on even in church. Reverence was reflected throughout, but the heavy, heavy, heaven help us tone was thankfully absent. The tropical garden within the alcove of the Church said it all. Melissa was sure to be in one of the small chapels lighting candles while saying the rosary, purifying herself for our reunion.

In the little gift shop I found a medallion of the Holy Spirit engraved as a dove with rays of paradise light surrounding its head.

Santana

I bought seven of them for the price of a days worth of rum and took them over to one of the candle alters, baptizing each one by dipping them into the hot wax while saying prayers for power as they dried. I kept in mind who I would give the first four to, then went anonymous on the other three for new friends who might come my way.

The first of the three appeared the very next day. Thomas from Sacramento had that look that said "how can I help you" when I first saw him walking my direction on Las Ramblas. I can't say I knew exactly what it was, but he had spiritual fire written all over him – the slow burner type. It would have been too silly not to stop him for a moment and introduce myself. He had been in town for a week now, fresh off a holiday love affair on the French Riviera and seriously considering staying in Barcelona to live with his new love, on her way here in two weeks time. We hit it off immediately, and his Spanish skills and knowledge of the city were excellent. He had heard of the Urantia Book from a biography on Elvis Presley, of all people. We got into it a bit at an excellent seafood stand that he had discovered. We fueled up on calamari for the dance floors we would hit that night. Besides the perfectly timed nap, this town did not know quit.

Along our way that afternoon, we ran into three other Americans rolling a piano around a corner close to the main drag of Las Ramblas. They were on their way to their spot to play for the crowds that evening. Their line-up consisted of drums, guitar and the piano player who sang. Real, down to earth fellas having a ball playing the Blues, making enough to live it up large for the summer and hone in on their own style. I suggested there might be room for a little diversity by offering my services so the singer could get out from behind the piano for a tune or two during the set. Of course they were game.

This I considered a small miracle; even attitudes between musicians could be put on hold here. We worked out a couple of numbers right there and then before we rolled to the promenade. I knew "Jealous Guy" by John Lennon and they showed me the changes for "Ain't no Sunshine When She's Gone" and "Hit the Road Jack." It

The Drunken Tourist

would have been nice to play some tune that didn't remind me of my Queen back home, but today I was trying to radio in Melissa instead, wherever she was.

After a song or two, I looked around in vain for the one girl that had temporarily derailed my Queen from relentlessly riding my soul. No such luck. I resigned myself to thinking it was my fate to continue alone with my heart in the States and my mind on the train from Paris.

I explored Barcelona for another few days, wandering through the cozy streets and the grand boulevards, to the fabulous fountains and the happy churches. The whole place was so wonderful that soon it started to get on my nerves. Inadvertently, I had conjured up quite the metropolitan resentment. The more splendid the night or the more carefree the neighborhood, the worse I felt. I just couldn't shake my ghost-girls no matter how hard I Rumba'd. Thomas was being an incredibly good sport, and if there was one place in the world you figure you could break a melancholy spell, it would be in Barcelona. Yet for me, the opposite was the case. Swimming in the sea of my own horseshit, I ended up getting obnoxiously drunk enough to collectively piss off half the town. The drunker I got, the more I felt rejected. Senoritas who saw me coming were crossing to the other side of the street in a hurry. Kids were suddenly bonding quickly with their parents. Old drunks were now noble patriarchs. And all these rejections obviously called for more of the drink. Sometime during the day I passed out, yet when I woke up, instead of suffering through the tremendous hangover, I went right back to my sloppy high. Soaked drunk and stinking, it was still hard for me to believe that I was not getting served at the bars of Barcelona. It must have been due to the fact that these regular folk just didn't have the inherent capacity or refined sensitivity to feel my noble pain. So just poor me another drink already.

Thomas finally suggested we go visit his Auntie who had a place in Mallorca. This certainly was not on the agenda, but the promise of a free and friendly roof over my head on an island in the middle of the Mediterranean sounded like just the ticket to recover for a couple of days. Once my legs returned to order, I'd come back and show them they couldn't keep a good drunk down.

Santana

The plan was to meet at the Columbus Monument at 10:30 – plenty of time to catch the 11:30 overnight boat to Mallorca. Meanwhile, Thomas would be gathering up his things and I would be sleeping off my lowball drunk of the night before. The timing could not have been better. The hostel I was staying at was full for the rest of the week, so I had to check out anyway, plus the cost of the ferry turned out to be less than the cost of two nights of sleep in town. I started to sweat it a little at 11:00 with Thomas nowhere to be found. At 11:15 I took the five minute walk to the ferry and boarded. Mallorca was my next stop, with or without him. I wasn't going to get deep into why he didn't show. It was probably my last drunk – the contradiction of someone promoting something like The Urantia Book while drinking like a fool might have been too much for him. Then again, maybe he had just decided to stay on in Barcelona. Either way, I had gone through enough rationalizations for the week in regards to other people's trips. If he was pissed at me, he had plenty of opportunity to lay it out. Whatever it was, I knew nothing tragic had happened to him. "Every snowflake is different," I told myself in New Yorkese. "Keep relying on other people for your security and this is what you get." What really pissed me off was that Thomas had my Urantia Book.

* * *

A group of ten or twelve were assembled on the outside deck of the ferry by the time I found my way up there. Chaise lounges were arranged against one of the ship's bulkheads, protected from the wind and the soot from the smokestack. The crowd was dominated by German and English backpackers with their rations of beer and wine already uncorked for the ride. I grabbed a lounger and got cozy for a sweet cruise under the stars.

After an hour or so out on the wide open waters, the guitars came out and the standards started to unravel me. Whoever this kid was playing "Old Man" by Neil Young had no business with it. Then "Positively 4th Street" completely pissed me off. I kept thinking about what a perfect scenario for suicide this particular boat trip could afford. I've heard drowning wasn't a bad way to go, but waiting to drown must be a real bitch. Still, the Milky Way

The Drunken Tourist

was all there, like I hadn't seen it for years, and the kid on the guitar gave it up soon enough. This left me ready for sleep. Despite the cold out on the deck, I scrunched up in my black trench and asked God for sleep or not.

* * *

The cathedral high on the hill greeted us as we pulled into the massive marina of Palma at dawn. How strange it was to see this giant, gothic church, looking so mighty and eternal, hovering over the luxury hotels and the hundreds of sailboats docked in the bay. The weather was perfect as I hoofed it to the center of town, then stopped at the tourist information office where they informed me that there was not one bed available in any hostel on the whole island. Yeah right. I took the free map and found a bed at the third place listed. I was soon to learn that dichotomy defined Mallorca. A little Barcelona, a little Bermuda, and a whole lot of criminals who had originally landed here to avoid extradition.

Everyone at the hostel was either working on a boat or waiting to set sail, so I headed to the marina through the ancient streets to find tall ships parked next to spanking new catamarans ready for Trans-Atlantic voyages.

Across the Avinguda Gabriel Roca from the marina I spied a jewel of a pool within the confines of a wrought iron gate in front of an expensive looking hotel. The doors to the gate were up a staircase, one full floor from street level which then led to the entrance of the luxury hotel overlooking the bay. There was a man made waterfall at one end of the water and a ping-pong table under the veranda next to the poolside bar – all fine ingredients for a pleasant afternoon.

Circling the hotel, I found the laundry room on the street level around the corner. There was one hamper overflowing with giant beach towels with the hotel logo in blue and green. If I had seen a maid, I would have asked for a fresh one, but nobody was around. A quick sniff test of one of the towels on top satisfied me with that refreshing aroma of chlorine and bleach. I borrowed it, took my pants and shirt off, tucked them in my day bag, and walked back around the corner and up to the gate in my big blue boxers– the

Santana

towel draped over my shoulders and my sunglasses on. I timed
my entrance just as a bellboy escorted a couple out the gate, and
headed straight past the ping-pong table to a deck chair in the sun.
Taking no chances, I laid out the towel on the lounger without
looking around and then dove right in. I figured I'd at least get a
swim out of the deal before somebody kicked me out. I made it all
the way underwater to the waterfall on the other side. God, that sun
felt good with the water massaging my back and neck. All further
explorations for the day would end here. I had come to Mallorca
to relax and that was what I was going to do, no matter how hard
it was to finally sit still for a while. The art of relaxation must have
something to do with money. Everybody poolside was so content
– just lounging around, tanning away. I had tried this before with
little success. Maybe that was it; with a little success you could
finally indulge in a really good tan.

So that's how they did it; first the work, then the tan. Then of
course, you have the ones whose work is the tan. Every time I lay out,
I just end up thinking about all the things I could be doing instead.

The only real challenge left in the current scenario was if I should
expose myself enough to risk playing a little ping-pong. Some people
might consider this a rich man's sport, but I had long ago developed
a mature game on an institutional level. The pressure of sun bathing
for almost an hour got me over there to the table, applauding some
decent returns. When the victor invited me to play, I warmed up lefty
and asked what he was drinking. The local rum punch sounded too
good not to bet a drink on the game, and whatever the two ended
up costing him, I was sure it was more than what my bed was for
the night. We finished off playing doubles with a kid looking on and
then it was back to the pool and the sauna. By four o'clock, I was off
slumming it for the evening.

The streets in the center of Palma were packed by the time I got
back. A quick change and I was off, hitting a number of pubs in the
center of town. Bold Germans and loud Brits dominated the scene in
and around the open air bars.

The vibe was very spring-break collegiate, soccer was on the telly,
and waves of hard rock worked their way out to the streets. The
Club Barcelona was the jazz joint situated in the heart of the district,

The Drunken Tourist

serving the strongest beer on the planet for about four bucks. So I splurged; my daily drink money hadn't even been touched yet. The Manhattan 6 was playing for the next two evenings. An East Village jazz band jamming in Mallorca? Well, why not? It went right along with the rest of the incredulousness of this place.

"Hey there, how are you?"

"Good evening; feeling fine, are we now?"

"By all means, by all means."

"Estabien, estabien."

This was the talk of the town. Everything was definitely "estabien." Another good "Hola" and I had to stop this one particular guy rambling down the street. He looked so happy I just couldn't resist. "What are you up to my friend?"

"We are headed to Le Clandestine, to hear some friends play. Care to join us?"

"By all means, sir," I replied. "Lead the way."

"Estabien, my friend, estabien," he proclaimed.

"Estabien, my friend," I confirmed. "For sure, it is. What is this Le Clandestine, a bar? This 'Le Clandestine…' I very much like saying the name, you know?"

"There are quite a few Le Clandestines in the neighborhood," he replied, "it is a bar that you wouldn't know was a bar unless you knew it was a bar, comprende?"

"Comprende, my friend; estabien, estabien."

The music I heard that night was a combination of Disco beats and Latin rhythms with Rock guitar. This was the sweet bitch called Mallorca all over again; trash and vaudeville, litter and luxury. The island as a whole wasn't that pretty, but in bed she was gorgeous. And this guy Gabriel? Where did he come from? He just kept this steady beam going all night long. People gravitated around him to drink from the open bar of his energy.

Gabriel, the man, lived in the attic of his aunt's neighbor's house. He split the utility bill with them every month to cover his rent. Primarily a guitarist and singer, he had just "received" a portable keyboard from a friend. By evening's end, I was climbing up the ladder to his comfortable nest where he fixed me some tea and showed me my spot where I would sleep on a piece of foam for the night.

Santana

Gabriel, the cosmic prankster, really lived in the moment. And man, did he have some tricks up his sleeve.

First thing in the morning we agreed that he was going to learn my tunes and we were going to go from Clandestine to Clandestine performing my wonderful songs to the amazed crowds of Mallorca. Then he came on like he was actually spiritually inspired with my particular slant on what God was up to. He let me go on and on with tales of beliefs and more beliefs as we toured around Palma.

By the end of the day, I had pretty much exhausted myself and was ready to go poolside to work on my tan. Gabriel, however, had other plans. We lugged the keyboard and his guitar to a decrepit façade in front of an old stone building, knocking three or four times before we were finally let in by a woman who looked like my lost Melissa's sister.

Isabella was an artisan of paper-mache, specializing in Salamanders for table tops and exotic fish that schooled in mobiles. Isabella's husband Danielo was more abstract, working in acrylics on canvas. These two, just like Gabriel, had no aspirations except to entertain the people they knew. At first I thought this was charmingly naïve of them; happy locals with no real ambition – thus no great talent. Yet they were very accomplished, with a house full of product to show for it. They were clearly quite content with doing their thing on a local level. Despite this, I tried to help out their quaint operation by working on the figures for import/export, Mallorca to New York, Palma to Soho. "You could get two hundred bucks apiece easy for these beauties," I remember saying to Isabella. It seemed like she didn't care about the money. She just delighted in my enthusiasm for her work.

Danielo was making grilled-cheese sandwiches while Gabriel set up the keyboards. Isabella rolled a beauty of a hashish cigarette. I accepted some local rum. Gabriel began humming a melody on top of a simple beat and baseline, then Isabella started to sing along in harmony. The song started to gather momentum when a middle aged couple appeared in the doorway and spontaneously joined us. I closed my eyes and hummed along for at least sixteen bars while Gabriel ventured a lyric:

The Drunken Tourist

You say you're fine
You say all is well
Estabien for a moment or two
But there's the train
And the promise of more
You say you're fine
and you know that you're lyin'

Our background harmonies worked their way in beautifully again, now joined by two more voices. I opened my eyes to find another couple had come in unannounced. We were now eight in the room, singing along with this same tune for what seemed like twenty times through. That's when it all started coming back to me. The fix was in – I was being transported back into a timeless space that I had first found many years ago on a guru's little boat in Sausalito.

There had been this same pairing of strangers as tonight, all looking oddly familiar, stopping by as if for no apparent reason other than to say hello, but instead, collectively reverberating the human arena apparently necessary to host this type of event. They asked silly questions to no one in particular that somehow threatened cherished beliefs of mine. Casual comments found me defending myself. When this scrambling revealed nothing defendable, a separation occurred where I was watching myself enact this charade. This went on for hours, until by dawn, I was down to the last bit of what was left of what I had thought was me, increasingly aware that I was undergoing some important initiation process. Layer upon layer of self-identification was exposed for the fraud it was, exposed by the very same self that was trying to save its own little life. The game was Truth vs. Everything Else, and the only player left on the "Everything Else" team was the fear of losing my core sense of identity.

Instinctively I knew I needed some authorization from my Creator to let go absolutely. I somehow figured the thing to do was to wait to surrender that last piece of me, if only the Christ would give me His blessing. But the sign did not come, so I refused to surrender my soul seed.

After repeated attempts to get me back into the process, all the guests eventually left from the boat early that morning. I was left with my host, present in the furthest and most sacred place of being I had ever been, waiting for my Christ, reeling in the bliss of cosmic citizenship.

I felt like I fell short. First, because I did not surrender that last part of me, and secondly because Christ did not give me any indication in that regard. Yet this did not taint my bliss. I walked off that boat and stayed in a rapture within the Eternal Kingdom of Now for the next forty-eight hours. All of nature was vibrating with the same cause. That cause resonated as Love – and I along with it. Physically, my body worked with this rhythm of life, a natural pulse and lean that I can still conjure up a little through my torso as I am writing this. Mentally, my mind was occupied to its complete satisfaction as an eyewitness. Spiritually... there was no spiritually, for to describe the experience as spiritual would imply a division that was no longer there. I had previously understood the term "spiritual" as a place separate from reality, and this was in no way true. In fact, the opposite may very well have been the case.

Emotionally, besides the sheer, unbounded joy of it, I was feeling compassion for people who were just walking along in their own business, oblivious to my newly found allegiance. And yet, once the initial bliss of the experience wore off, this feeling of compassion changed itself into a cloak of loneliness.

Tonight, Gabriel was pulling the same number. I was allowed to sufficiently unravel myself and my cherished beliefs in order to let it all go. Once again, I returned to this swell of peace, well satisfied – my mind happily delegated to bare witness to this same Love. Tonight I was determined to share this rediscovered place of joy wholeheartedly with the good people around me. This was certainly no chore. Gabriel knew what was going on, and it didn't even matter if everybody else around knew it or not. This was an all inclusive conspiracy. We were all here to harmonize.

How do you possibly say thank you to someone who leads you to lead yourself to such a sacred place? And how do you stay there – or at least execute a decent re-entry? To keep the Kingdom in mind while performing the immediate task at hand has got to be one of the

The Drunken Tourist

greatest arts of living. Nobody could possibly maintain that quality of life, or could they? When inspired, I could hold the Present in mind for maybe a few minutes while I did the simplest of things. Then I would go about my day and forget all about it.

Tonight I was determined to exchange this currency of pulsating power into the bank of my oversoul before I forgot. This soul pilot of mine could do a much better job of carburating this power into action than little old me. At least I had learned this much through all my book studies. "Striking step with eternity" was now my charge.

All those years ago I had made the terrible mistake of resenting so much of what I did not understand. I translated this resentment into a refueling of my propensity towards overindulgence. Tonight I didn't want to justify any of it. Tonight I wanted to concentrate on this state of grace, one foot in front of the other.

Earlier in the day, I had made arrangements with the Club Barcelona to do a short set before the featured act of the evening. Gabriel urged me to go. He said this was as good a time as any to "get with it."

"What you hold as sacred, is sacred," he whispered.

My thought then added, "If it is sacred, it is becoming real."

I flew out the door to play one of the best performances of my life. Absolute resolutions on the piano were now not as critical. The game was in the improv; I could watch myself play and take delight in it. Page 351 of The Glass Bead Game was now coming to life. I saw the attitude of my own ego towards the situation "with serenity and a clean tempo." Now holding back from "thrusting your way in to the center of the world," I entered into "the center of my own individuality." What a blast.

Ina had been listening. Tall, blond and German, she approached me as I approached the bar after my little set.

"Are you from England?" she ventured.

"No, I'm from the States," I explained. Although "from the States," always sounded a bit corny to me, I had found it worked much better than the thoroughly ostentatious reply of "I'm from New York but I live in L.A."

Santana

So Ina and I got to talking over another one of those excellent brews that were now on the house. She was an optometrist, just getting over some sailor that had recently left her high and dry. I was a piano player who had just had a mini-Samadhi, feeling the tug of her charms. It's amazing how easily you can find a little action once you really don't need it that bad. "I'm going back to a friend's Le Clandestine tonight," I announced, "I would like you to join me; can you come along?"

"Of course," she replied. "I would love to get out of this place… everybody here knows me and my ex. We've had some ugly scenes in here."

"Is he due back in town?"

"Yes," she sighed, "apparently he is already back, but he hasn't looked me up. I believe he must be avoiding me."

"Well tonight I will forget my ex if you forget yours, O.K.?"

"Yes, yes," she sad. "Let's enjoy ourselves for the time being."

"Here's to the Time Being," I toasted.

"To the Time Being," she concurred.

We eased into a comfortable walk through the crowds toward Isabella and Danielo's place. "This has got to be it," I explained as I kept knocking; "I was just here."

"I know a great bar down the street," Ina suggested, "the bands there are usually very radical."

"Well, let's go then," I said. "I'm sure they will be around, we'll come back and check later."

An hour after we had settled in, I excused myself for a minute to check back on my friends. Still, no answer.

By the time I got back to Ina's bar, she was liplocked with her sailor man. God, they looked great together. This had to be some kind of cosmic pop quiz. I approached them during a break in their action and introduced myself, then said goodnight. The first steps out the door were the hardest as I walked on, a good citizen of the universe again, humming Gabriel's melody. Apparently being alone was the current exchange rate for this state of grace. I thanked that sailor and the rest of the navigators on board. "What you hold as sacred, is sacred," went the sea-song, "If it is sacred, it is becoming real."

The Drunken Tourist

The route I was to take was of no concern of mine for the rest of the evening – the only places I wasn't going were down those same emotional routes I was so sick of.

Between Gabriel's Pow-Wow high and Ina's Ferris Wheel letdown, I was prime for a good wreck. I needed a Plan B. I needed to compartmentalize. As stupid as Plan A was, it was simple: I knew I moved well without hesitation. Then, when I was bad, I wanted to be good; when I was good, I wanted to be bad.

It ended up that I never saw Isabella or Danielo or even Gabriel again. I went by Gabriel's place three times the next day before his neighbor finally let me in. There was no sign of him anywhere, and my Spanish couldn't get any kind of discernable explanation out of the old woman. Gabriel had disappeared on me, but his song and spirit were stuck in my head.

* * *

The train to Sollier was recommended as a must while on the island, so I took the first one out of Palma in the morning. The antique train rambled its way out of town with all its windows open, then slowly climbed the hills through the chilliest tunnel I've ever been through. We emerged on cliff's edge, revealing a vista of stupendous mountaintops surrounding a lush valley wherein the city of Sollier was tucked. I imagined this place as an ideal convention center for seraphic hosts on business or pleasure. It was also one of those places that begged for intimate company.

At the station, the train line connected with a trolley headed down to the beach. The cove was sparkling enough, but the crowds and the beach were disappointing compared to the view from above, so I headed straight back on the trolley to the train station.

All train compartments were empty when I boarded with a good twenty minutes to wait before departure time. I looked around and then inside. To my surprise there was still that same fat hole sitting there in the middle of my heart, plain as day. And here I was thinking I was all put together now, in my tidy little compartments with wisdom's whip on call. How long had I been walking around like this? What a fashion flaw. Plan B should have taken care of it. Yet this hole couldn't

Santana

be filled reminiscing on the best views or the best times or the best realizations or even with the best rock and roll. Maybe this empty place came to me only when I stopped moving; sitting still seemed to get me leaning towards that twilight melancholy, sighs shading the simplest responses... alone, thinking how no one was coming. No one was coming. Not even Alexander, the one that always gave me something to look forward to, the one that understood me as "one of us." Forget the unfaithful women and unreliable friends, together my boy and I could build a big day from scratch.

That would be our family's crest in the hall of records – the Santana clan spinning an island from the salt in the middle of the sea. We would sing our little songs as we spun our little island 'til birdbrains would fly by laughing and try to shit on us. We'd dance on that bird shit, grinding it into the salt, while the sun and rain danced with us all the way to the bank of brand new territory.

Today there was plenty of territory but no Alex, and no wonderful Queen of our island. Nobody coming. There was only a desire to share the curious shape of the latches on the windows of the train that distracted me while I waited; a simple desire to share a simple item with someone that didn't care about the latches on the windows, but cared that I noticed them and listened anyway.

* * *

Moments before the end of our short time together, Ina had recommended the Hotel Cuba in Palma. The private room was a welcome relief from the hostels I had been settling on for the past few weeks and the hotel itself was only a few hundred yards from my favorite pool side ping-pong table. Mentioning Ina's name to the owner might have helped get the price down, but what the fellow behind the desk had forgotten to mention was that they were demolishing the building next door.

The wrecking ball's siesta was the only chance for sleep. Downright cranky, I decided that afternoon to check out early and catch the boat back to Barcelona and then catch the train that evening.

The ferry ride proved no better for rest. The deck was cold and the bar was closed. The top deck had a lounge area inside with sofa

The Drunken Tourist

chairs scattered throughout. Pulling two of them together made a precarious bed. As soon as I laid out, all the change in my pocket fell into the crevice of one of the chairs. As I dug for the loose change, my hand closed on a small, black, zippered up pouch stuck in the crease, hundreds of pesetas folded neatly inside.

Even though I suck at math, I knew right then I had at least doubled my total net worth. There was no identification of any kind within the pouch, and even if there was, I would have probably taken the majority of the cash and left the I.D.

Once safely off the boat in Barcelona, I counted out something like the equivalent of $400US! Money, the old mood changer, exchanged my stride for a swagger as I walked pig-heaven into the city, ready to afford one good day back in Barcelona before the train ride east.

First stop was Gaudi's La Familiar, the happiest church I've ever seen. The admission price would have been quite manageable today, but they weren't charging. The insides were under construction and it could stay that way forever as far as I was concerned.

Next was the Picasso Museum, featuring his greatest doodles and only one canvass that really got me. Again, I was ready to pay, but they weren't charging at the time I showed up. The gift shop was the most interesting room in the place, but nothing struck me as worthy of transport.

With all this money burning up in my pocket, I treated myself to an excellent meal of wine and fish, then dozed off on a bench along the promenade before making my way back to the train station.

* * *

The aisles on the old train were crammed with whole families shuffling around for a spot to squat in the aisles. I tried to squeeze by a few fellas with their backpacks for a space to sit near the far end of the car.

"No room that way, mate," I heard one guy say casually as I approached.

"There's no room the other way either," I answered, exasperated.

"Looks like you're stuck here with us then," he said, face in face.

"Right here next to the bathrooms? How convenient," I sighed.

"We'd be happy to watch your bags for you while you freshen up a bit, dear," the second guy chimed in.

Santana

"Is my breath that bad?" I whispered. "It says you're not supposed to drink the water in the bathrooms on the train; do you suppose it's O.K. for brushing?"

"Go on and take it like a man," said punk number one with a smile.

Punk number two then shouted out, "For the love of God, man, do it for the children!" and everyone spit out a laugh.

"For the children," punk number one repeated in mock piety.

I lowered my head down in shame, then looked up and whispered, "We are the World."

Then, of course, we had to start humming that melody without knowing the words. The tune soon turned into: "We are the world, We are the thirsty, We are the ones who really need a drink or we'll get nasty."

Our area in the middle of the two train cars had the two punks from Australia, three Greeks, two girls from Israel, and Martha from Brooklyn. Within ten minutes we were all imbibing on the Greeks' wine and my rum. It was one of those situations where nobody hesitated sharing from the start, otherwise it would have been awkward.

Martha and I got to talking about New York while we stood against the wall near the bathroom. My new buds, Lenny and Roland were standing up in the middle of the two cars talking to the Greeks that were sitting in the stairwell of the train leading to the door. The girls from Israel were squatting against the beginning of the corridor with their luggage leaning against the accordion partition between the cars. The train was trying spastically to get rolling. It would gather some speed, then it would brake and bolt radically enough that the luggage would start to topple before we lunged for it, stumbling into each other. This happened twice before Lenny suggested we prepare for the next barrage of herky-jerks by putting all the luggage in the middle between the cars where the axle rotated, then everyone could claim a fair piece of the wall for themselves. This sounded plausible enough, but the next time the train braked, Martha and I fell forward into the pile of luggage separating us from Roland and Lenny, who somehow managed to catch our fall before we hit the floor. Now we were sort of stuck leaning in a huddle, arms on shoulders, steadying each other over our belong-

The Drunken Tourist

ings, waiting for the next jerk of the train. Lenny quickly assumed the role of the quarterback: "O.K. now team," he began. "We can take this train. Let's just go with the motion."

"Let's go with the motion," Roland repeated. And with that we got a collective bounce going as the train started to roll along again. As we gathered speed our bounce grew. The faster the train chugged, the higher our stretch went. We swayed together on a turn. We swelled higher still before the train did one of its violent jerks, causing Lenny to break from the pack and land on his ass on top of the luggage. What a score.

"Let's do it again," Martha demanded.

The momentum started and again we followed with our gypsy dance; "I...feel...like...I got...the train.. .by the balls..." Lenny exclaimed to the rhythm of the train.

"Keep it going, keep it going," I chimed in. "Here we go, here we go, we got it hummin' now."

"Humma humma, Humma humma," we chanted with the chugga.

"Hey hey hey, HEY!" the Greeks answered with their mantra.

One of them opened the stairwell door and the world hit fast-forward –

Shugga CHUGGA, Shugga CHUGGA,

"Humma HUMMA, Humma HUMMA"

"Hey hey hey, HEY! Hey hey hey, HEY!"

The Israeli girls got in on the last "HEY!"

"Shut the fuckin' door!" yelled Roland.

"Shut the Fuckin' Door!... Shut the Fuckin' Door!".. we all got raving... with the same rhythm... of the fuckin' train.

With the door fucking shut, the ride started to smooth out a little, but we still didn't break. The hum was in us now – here was that energy again that centered in the middle of my torso. It could have been coming from the train and could have been coming from us or it could have been us and the train and the Spirit and whatever else was working and who the fuck cares? We were rolling.

"Do you feel the energy in your chest?" I asked the group.

"I feel it," said Lenny.

"I got it too," echoed Martha.

"Let's break and see if it's still there," suggested Roland.

"Yes, let's break," said the Greek who had joined in, as he dropped his arms.

I sat down against the wall and took a deep breath. Martha opened the door of the bathroom, wiped the toilet seat off, and sat on the bowl with the door open.

"How are you feeling?" I asked her.

"Great," she sighed. "Like I'm on speed or something."

"Me too," I answered. "I was exhausted, but now I'm feeling great. What's happening with you, Lenny?"

"I'm charged up," he replied. "I'm really charged up."

The Greeks passed another bottle around and the Israeli girls made room for Martha on the floor next to them as somebody had to use the bathroom. I got down in the stairwell and opened the door again to check out the fleeting neighborhood. The group immediately voiced their concern for my safety, so I shut the fucker to keep the peace.

Lenny, Roland, and Martha were connecting to Paris. The Greeks and the Israeli girls were going as far as Genoa. I ended up lending Martha the equivalent of fifteen dollars that she promised to pay me back by letting me stay at her apartment in Brooklyn for a night when I got to New York. Before we arrived at the station in Marseille we decided to group together again for a little encore. The train was rolling along at a fairly smooth clip at this point, but still, with a little more footwork, we were able to sufficiently conjure up a more subdued concoction of the earlier brew. As in a good night in the sack, the second round was more meaningful– more intimate in certain regards. When we got off the train we hugged each other goodbye, looking for and receiving a last taste of that shared feeling that none of us were likely to forget.

We never did see the conductor the whole ride.

DANUBE
AMUSEMENT PARK
NANA'S SHOP
$ # HOOD
A FINE SLICE
ST. STEVIES
PROMENADE
CASINO
PROMENADE
PROMENADE
CLUB HAVANA
PEPE'S HOOD
UP THE HILL
TROLLEY
MOZART
OPERA HOUSE
VISITORS
NEPTUNE & CO.
FREUD
MODERN ART
LIBRARY
JIMMY D'S
BUDDHA & SUPERMODELS
THE STATUE AGAINST THE PLAQUE
STROLLING
RUINS
A FINE BEER IN THE SHADE
GUCCI HOOD
THE SEXIEST BILLBOARD
MUSEUMS
PALACE
CHRISTIANA
UNIVERSITY WAY
MELODY
OUR LITTLE PUB
THE MIRROR BAR
CHRISTIANA'S NEIGHBORHOOD
THE SEXIEST BILLBOARD AGAIN
PALACE

Vienna

Take Manhattan around 59th Street from Park Avenue west to Lincoln Center, add a taste of Prague and a good serving of Paris and you get an idea of what a fine city Vienna is.

There was a quiet dignity pervading the streets that so many of the greats had called home as I passed a statue of Nietzsche, then the Opera House and the Casino, then on to the civilized swarm of St. Stephens. I felt perfectly comfortable in my suit and tie, high on life and good bourbon, passing beautiful women everywhere, most of them dressed to the nines. This town was downright elegant.

On the way towards the Club Havana, I found myself alone on one of the side streets. As was my custom, I started humming a little number a few decibels lower than what I would belt out in a similar situation on the streets of New York. A woman with long brown hair and dressed all in black turned a corner on the other side of the same narrow street I was walking on before I could turn it down a notch.

"Well, don't stop on my account," she said from across the street as she kept on walking. "What's that you're singing, anyways?"

"Nothing really," I answered. "Just a little melody floating around."

"This town is famous for melody floating around, you know."

"That's what I hear," I said without thinking.

"So you're really a bad comedian then," she laughed, still walking along with me from the other side of the street.

"Yeah, that's it," doing my best impression of a routine I remembered from Saturday Night Live. "That's it, I'm a… comedian tonight, yeah…you got it…" And with that I crossed the street and introduced myself. Her name was Christiana and she looked strong.

"I am on my way towards another Mint Julip, would you care to join me?" I asked, formally.

"I would be delighted, sir," she responded in tone. We walked along while Christiana good naturedly cracked on my half-drunken condition until we came to the club which was a few blocks down past the Opera House. "I've been wanting to go in here for some time now," she commented as we arrived at the door. "How did you hear about it?"

"I was invited about two hours ago by a new found friend," I answered as we made our way up the stairs and then back down another flight to the bar. My buddy greeted us on our arrival, pouring us a generous dose of some vodka concoction we had to try.

The dance floor was a mix of the old pros looking a bit too contrived doing their old pro maneuvers, the intermediates trying to do the old pro thing and having no fun at all, and then the amateurs, with their mock posturing, stepping all over each other, then laughing together in perfect synch while getting it going for a few bars at a time.

Despite the abundance of beauties and alcohol, I was true to my date, looking towards her in strict tempo while my legs responded to the blessed Salsa. We met Juan Carlos from Chile, Genevieve and Richard from France, and Carly from the States now living in Vienna, whom Christiana bonded with well enough for Juan and I to sneak out and toot a good one and one. Consequently, I hit one of those sweet plateaus of a combination high that comes to me once every 232 times that I get high; the other 231 in between pretty much spent on obliterating everything that is working in my life in search of Old Number 232.

Thanks to the music, there was no room for the usual resume gibberish. Christiana was as bad as I was on the dance floor and we had a ball not trying to improve. We even got into coaxing other fun loving amateurs for a quick switch of partners to do a few brave new twirls in the middle of the songs. The whole business of the evening was run in the strictest concern towards absolute spontaneity.

It was also quite apparent that everybody there had money. Drinks and promises of new acquaintances turning into beneficial friend-

The Drunken Tourist

ships were flying off the bar. Within a few hours, I knew half the bar better than I knew Christiana .

We didn't have a chance to get to talking until after we closed the joint and were walking to the trolley. By that time it was too late. We started making out around the first corner we turned. It took us a half an hour to make it the three blocks to the train stop. Waiting for the train was the gentlemanly thing to do, along with taking the ride, walking her to her apartment house, climbing up the stairs and into her bed. Christiana was a fine and steady lover. She whispered Austrian to me as I moved in and out. Without knowing a word, it all sounded so much more motivating to me than any attempt I've ever heard in English to vocally balance the dirty and the tender. At any rate, we pretty much broke through the language barrier with the universal moans of going over the top before we both passed out.

* * *

"My chest is killing me," were the first words out of my mouth first thing in the morning. The girl didn't say a word. She got up, put on her robe, went out to the bathroom and in a minute appeared with a glass of juice in one hand and a stethoscope in the other.

"Sit up for a minute," she said gently.

"Why certainly, doctor," I joked as I leaned forward.

"Your health is not a joke. I could see from last night that you don't take care of yourself; now let me listen," she said before she did the elementary school infirmary routine. Finally, she sighed, "Well, it's probably your lungs looking for some fresh air because your heart sounds fine."

"I think I'm in excellent shape for 57, don't you?" I said.

"Very funny. I think you wouldn't joke if you spent a day with me at the hospital," she replied.

"You work at a hospital?" I asked.

"Yes," she replied, "I am in my third year of a residency, specializing in post-surgery rehabilitation in cardiovascular therapy."

"You devil," I said. "All last night you led me to believe you were a dance instructor… how could you?"

"I didn't want to intimidate you, that's all," she laughed.

"You mean on the dance floor or with the medical lingo?" I asked.

"What's lingo?" she asked.

"You know…" I smiled, "how you were talking in bed last night."

"You know," she said, "you are a fucking terrible comedian."

We held a good look together until she started muttering something under her breath in Austrian again as I got her back under the covers.

Half asleep I heard, "don't forget to lock the door on your way out," as Christiana left me to rest while she was off to the hospital for the day. We were to meet downtown at 7:00 and meanwhile I could ring Reneé and look to place a Urantia book at the National Library. On the other hand, Juan had given me his phone number last night, so I could ring him, probably get high and then hit the Casino across the street from the Opera House. I decided to go back to sleep then get up and try to do it all. There was an uncertain comfort as I curled up under her covers thinking that in the space of less than twenty-four hours I had myself a little life going in Vienna.

It was good to see Reneé again. A friend met again on the road is twice the friend, indeed. He liked my new scruff of a beard and told me I looked more relaxed. I liked that, and told him it was only because "my feelings were now my own." We had a quick coffee and hopped on his Honda 650 to peruse the town. It was a nice transition from the go-girl red bicycle route of Berlin.

We made it to the amusement park area around the Danube, which was dead, then had a brew and continued on to the outskirts of town to his university's campus. Vema, his girlfriend, met us for a quick lunch between her classes, promising to get together later that evening. Reneé and I headed back to the center of town and parked the bike to walk to St. Stephen's Square.

Across the street, in the shadows of the cathedral, we met Chester, maybe 22 years old, originally from Chicago, now happily stranded in Vienna, creating large pastel drawings on the sidewalks. His work featured Buddhas and supermodels, symbols of Science and Celestials all dancing with fine symmetry in brilliant colors. He had just spent a year in Venice Beach, of all places, living about three miles from my house in Los Angeles. You could plainly see he was taking in good revenue today from the donations of people passing by. "In the States," he explained, "everybody would slow down to look at the

The Drunken Tourist

work, then say something like, 'really nice,' and keep walking. Like I was a government subsidized public service or something. There was always somebody who would throw me a couple of bucks, but everybody else would ask me some stupid question instead like, 'How long did this take you?' or 'Do you have this for sale?' Knowing, of course, that I didn't have it for sale and I was making it on the sidewalk right in front of them. Here, everybody that stops gives me a little something. It all adds up and the police don't usually hassle me."

He had a good spot alright, so Reneé ran to the store for some brews and we spent the rest of the day hanging out around the work in progress, filling in spaces that the artist allowed us to fill in under his direction and talking with the curious passing by. When Chester's local lady showed up with her girlfriend, we had a nice little group in a nice little corner of Vienna for the afternoon. I loved the fact that this guy truly had the ideal craft to work anywhere, making a buck while making a good scene. I had a little trouble with the fact that the rain would come and wash it all away, but once again, I was being shown firsthand that it was all about the beauty of the day.

Christiana found Reneé and I well tanked when she met us at Nietzsche's statue at 7:00. I half expected she might be pissed finding me in such a state, but instead she was just happy to see me. Just happy to see me? Imagine that. Now why couldn't I just fall in love with her? As soon as I asked myself that question, I looked at her and knew it wasn't going to happen. And ain't that a bitch. So I kissed her like mad anyway, losing the message but holding on to the messenger.

We went pub crawling around town with Reneé and Vema that night, having a splendid time despite the asterisk that could have been mistaken for our star only a few hours earlier. Watching Reneé and his girl stargazing didn't help. Yet it was all perfect for the moment. It just wasn't perfect enough for me, Mr. Limbolover.

Surprisingly or not, our sex was even better than before. Maybe the release of the love pressure helped. Christiana knew what was up, and apparently had more of the ability available to enjoy our time together than I did. Chances were pretty good that this was her expectation in the first place, but these things were much better left unsaid. As my pal Reneé had mentioned in Berlin, "there are some things I don't need to know." It was just me looking for more than necessary.

The following evening we got completely decked out, looked up Juan, did great coke, had great sex in half our great clothes, put our great clothes back on, had a great time losing only something like forty bucks collectively at the Black Jack tables, saw half of a great Opera (though we should have stayed for the whole show), then ended up back at Club Havana doing the blessed Salsa thing until we closed the joint again.

I remember hitting the men's room and looking in the mirror saying something like, "It's not going to get much better than this, here. Why aren't you satisfied?" I was with the lions again, this time feeling resigned to it, going through a quick perusal of another 231 highs just to say "fuck you" to good old Number 232. It was back to Truth vs. Everything Else, and Everything Else was certainly not looking too great, looking back at me in that mirror.

Welcome to Krakow

Krakow

She looked back once without breaking stride. There would be no teary-eyed farewell, only a good hug and a hard kiss. She left me with a postcard and a pack of smokes before I climbed aboard the overnight train to Poland. Struggling to reciprocate, I had to give up my membership card for the Club Havana that I was going to keep as a souvenir. I felt selfish that I hadn't planned it that way. She wrote about burning my candles at both ends and how "people" would take me more seriously if I took better care of myself. It was a well thought out farewell.

* * *

The story goes that before the Nazis invaded during World War II, the town collectively decided to evacuate. Once the Panzer division rolled in, legend has it that the commanders thought the city had already been taken by another one of their divisions, so they didn't fuck with the town at all. Thus we have an intact Krakow today.

This morning looked much the same as it might have looked back then. There were only three or four people at the station, all the ticket windows were closed, and nobody spoke English. I saw a hotel's light on across the square and went in to inquire on the rates. The clerk there was gracious enough to direct me to a hostel only a few blocks away.

The town was uncomfortably quiet as I followed the trolley tracks in the direction advised. There was no telling where the actual city was, or if there even was one at all. I walked along the curve of the tracks until I came upon a colossal four story, rectangular building that happened to be the hostel I was looking for. The isolated walk to the Jan Pol Hostel left me with the impression that at the very least there was nothing to be afraid of here in Krakow.

I was assigned a bed in a room with three other fellows, all traveling alone and just getting ready for their day when I arrived. Erik was some sort of a physicist from England who was working in Berlin. Then there was Fritz, a journalist from Brussels, who worked for some left wing magazine in Amsterdam. And finally Jeremy, on break from college in Seattle and a huge baseball fan. Jeremy and Erik planned to start the day at one of the internet cafés around the city center. Fritz was off to the library for the morning, which motivated me to ask directions for a visit I would later pay to the acquisitions department to place a Urantia Book there.

The hostel was located just outside the city center, and this center was all the Krakow I needed to know. On the other side of the ancient stone wall surrounding the old city, the cobblestones started to wind into narrow streets devoid of cars and Nike logos, the McDonalds arches easy to avoid. Most everybody I passed looked forward to eye contact and friendly nods. The center square had the marketplace in full swing when I arrived there for a late breakfast.

Food was even cheaper here than I had found in Prague, at about one quarter the price I could have easily paid in Vienna if I hadn't been so fortunate there. Financially, I was king again, and I set about to share the wealth as soon as possible, tipping generously at the breakfast table, which I was to find out later was not necessary. Within the hour, I realized I had found myself a new bastion for the now sacred 1.5 Second Rule and the new champion of the now confirmed international economic indicator: the price of a cold beer served at a table in the sun by a smiling local beauty.

The jazz joint in the heart of the city center square was just starting to buzz by the time I arrived to inquire about a happy hour gig. From what I gathered, the owner would be in by three that afternoon, and if I wanted to play, I could wait while they fed me a strong local brew. Maybe the barkeep thought I was already booked for an engagement, maybe not, but either way it was one more language barrier advantage coming my way.

Three pints later, I was auditioning on stage to fill in for some trio from Warsaw that hadn't shown up last night. After my standard flam-

The Drunken Tourist

boyant warm up routine, we agreed that I could play an early set if the other band showed and two sets if they didn't. The owner didn't want to pay me anything, so we settled on the obvious: simply extend the bar tab for the day. It was, as they say, my "Welcome to Krakow."

Wandering outside the circle of the inner city, I found a baby diner that served me six dumplings, two breaded chicken cutlets with potatoes and beets for a grand total of maybe three bucks, no tipping possible. Still further on the periphery, I found an outdoor bar that consisted of six tables surrounding a chilled keg of beer. The pint was about a buck, and again, no tipping was considered.

The rhythm of the town picked up tempo as twilight set in on my way to meet the fellows from the Jan Pol at a bar I only remember as called "Go." Before the first vodka of the evening could settle in, Jeremy came rushing in all excited about the pennant race back home. Nobody cared except me, but of course it was another cause to celebrate. The spirit of home run records would be alive and well as we proceeded to tear the bar up that night as if it was the last game of the World Series.

This bar had everything. Located at the southeast corner of the square, it attracted a mix of tourists and locals. The price of chilled vodka was sacrificed at two bucks a shot, managed by the cutest Polish blonde I had seen all day. Their monstrous music selection was listed in full by song on the menu, along with ten different kinds of dumplings, and requests were tallied at the bar according to consensus. Spectators were stationed at long wooden tables at either end of the two large rooms that made up this ancient dugout. The whole place must have been an underground cave dwelling years ago. Off in left field was a small stage with house congas waiting.

Towards the bathrooms was the internet room with maybe eight boxes working. Give me a fold-out bed in the back and I could have spent a winter here, hibernating with the blonde behind the bar. Fritz turned out to be an excellent drinking buddy, keeping right up with me, round for round. His eye was on an Australian redhead, while the rest of us were enjoying the drunken transformation of Erik the Physicist into Erik the Philosopher.

At about nine, I had to slip out to the jazz joint to pull off an hour set that stayed fresh and loose for at least eighteen minutes. The numbers were met with such polite applause it irritated me enough to grab a microphone for a slapstick version of "Jealous Guy." The end of the number and thus the end of the set was met with more polite applause. Thankfully, the tardy trio from Warsaw had showed up to spare me another hour.

"Go" was almost in full swing when I returned, and I was too charged to settle for anything less than a wholesale drunken riot. Prince was on the menu, and "I Want to Be Your Lover" was soon followed by "Little Red Corvette" The tables were moved back against the wall to make room for a dance floor. There would be no bopping along in place or leaning up against anything while Fritz and I did our part to rally the crowd. It was, however, my voluptuous barmaid who was the real catapult towards pandemonium, coaxing half the girls in the bar to follow her lead.

"Middle of the Road," by the Pretenders was then served with The Clash at high volume before Iggy Pop's "Lust for Life" and the Stones' "Tumbling Dice" brought the whole bar together in a collective bounce, screaming our fucking lungs out. So what if the crowd really didn't know the words, so what if I was too old for this type of shit, these Poles had endurance on their side and had me in a complete sweat spinning around in my shirt tails during the verse then back to the bounce for the choruses.

You bet that pulsating Power of the Present was involved. That power was starting to become more and more easily identified. It was apart from, but still in league with euphoria, and no longer to be confused with just being loaded. I was now looking out for this spirit no matter where, no matter what.

Life was so damn good that evening I decided to call my Queen back home and try to talk to her for the first time in almost four months.

"Hello?" she answered.

"Hello, my Queen, how are you?"

"Oh my God, is it you?"

"Yes, it's me," I said softly. "I'm calling you from Krakow."

"You're calling me from a crackhouse?"

"No," I laughed, "I'm calling you from Poland – Krakow, Poland."

"You're in Poland? We have been looking for you everywhere. I

The Drunken Tourist

went to your place, and nobody was there. I even called the jails looking for you, my dahrling."

When she called me dahrling it was all over. I melted.

"Are you in love with anyone these days?"

"Oh God," she said, "I am still loving you." And with that, she
started to cry.

And that was it. For all intensive purposes, my heart was back in
hock. Despite the sense of vindication for all my feelings for the past
110 days since we had been apart, I knew as soon as I hung up the
phone that the call could have waited. I had turned a corner and
was now back peddling into that dangerous neighborhood I knew I
couldn't handle. This was all confirmed by spending the majority of
the next day at the bar, writing her a three part letter while nursing
the morning after hangover with hot beers and lemon. All those twilights with her in mind were now settling in like Nitrous Oxide before
the dentist's drill. No amount of anesthesia, however, could have
possibly prepared me for what I was to see the following day.

* * *

Two bits of advice if you ever plan to go to Auschwitz: 1) Bring a
friend. If you don't have one handy, make one on the bus ride there.
2) Eat before you go. The only chance I got to try to eat anything was
in the middle of the day, taking the shuttle bus from Auschwitz 1 to
Auschwitz 2. Thank goodness all I had was a nectarine and a dough-
nut – anything more substantial would have completely shamed me.
The curators were very matter of fact when we walked in. They
explained the recommended routes and emphasized the movie to
be shown at one o'clock. Fritz and Jeremy made the trip, with Erik
absolutely refusing to go. Fritz proved to be an excellent companion
for the tour. He took his time, thus slowing me down, while holding
his comments to a minimum. He took a journalistic approach to the
experience and I adopted his tone.

The cynical inscription "Arbeit macht frei" (Work brings freedom)
hangs above the main gate as you enter. Against the kitchen building next to the gate was where the band played marches to muster
the prisoners to work. They had made a routine of playing songs
to people crying to death. There is a photograph in one of the first

buildings depicting this scene. The expressions on the faces of two SS officers look like they are two bullies in school taunting a disabled kid while they take his wheelchair for a joyride. The mugshots of the prisoners did not startle me. There was no defiance or fear in their faces – they were blank. The impression was that they were protecting their souls by concentrating on a place within themselves that was far enough away to create a critical numb. On the second floor you enter a room with a glass case running the length of the room. At first I thought it was a massive rat's nest, but it was human hair – the remains of bales upon bales of prisoner's hair, once cut to make haircloth. I had never even heard of haircloth. This was my first clue to the enormity of the death camp. The next room had two other similar glass cases, one full of luggage from the victims, another with tooth brushes and children's hair brushes. And all this was just the small amount left from what the Nazis didn't have time to destroy.

In the cellars were the ovens. The adjoining rooms had stalls where they would pack in the victims for days. The space was so tight that no one could sit or lay down. They had to stand up – naked, cold, face to face, waiting. Some would work until they died, some would be used for experiments, some would be sent to the gas chambers, while others, for the sake of convenience, would be taken outside against the execution wall and shot. According to the guide, during the worst of it, the Nazis were having a hard time disposing of all the human ashes from the incinerators. The film was a comfort compared to the images presented around the death camp. A cup of coffee afterwards was enormously civilized. No one said a word on the shuttle bus to Auschwitz 2 – the camp at Birkenau, built by the prisoners of Auschwitz 1. The train tracks run under the main watchtower straight through the camp, maybe 250 yards to the far end. Then the tracks just stop. This is where they unloaded the new arrivals. They were separated according to those that were deemed useful for work and those who were not. The ones too old or too weak or too crippled were told that they could finally shower. Then they herded them into the gas chambers that even had shower heads along with the gas vents to fool the victims until the very end. The Nazis didn't want the rest of the camp to know what was happening. Again, they had trouble trying to discard the remains.

Fritz and Jeremy went off to view the ponds where the ashes were

The Drunken Tourist

tipped, while I found a seat near the woods. Something was rustling on the other side of the barbed wire fence… yet I didn't feel any spirits. I felt odd – not capable of understanding, not able to relate as much as I wanted to.

Towards the women's barracks there was a group of thirty young-sters in blazing white and blue sweatshirts walking together with the flag of Israel catching the sun like a mirror in their midst. I hurried to catch up and join them. They welcomed me silently as they placed lit candles in the barracks along the way back to the watchtower. That was enough. I crossed the street and sat in a cab until Fritz and Jeremy appeared, ready to go.

Upon our return to the warmth of Krakow, all discussions on the excursion were meager, at best. We left the impressions of the day pretty much alone after a few awkward attempts to summarize the experience over the same meal at the same baby diner I had found two days ago. The next stop was obviously vodka, chilled.

Venice

"Bon Giorno," she said at the door to the restoration shop at the corner of the square.

"Bon Giorno," I responded. "Do you speak any English?"

"Yes, yes… please come in already," she offered. "You have been listening to the music, yes."

"Yes," I said. "Gershwin is one of my favorites."

"Prego. I play this all the time; I love my Porgy and Bess," she said with another smile as I walked into the front room of the shop. The music had been sweeping through the square all morning, which was different for this part of Venice – such a quiet place. "Please, take your time, I must finish up in the back," she said, and with that, left me alone in the middle of centuries of antiques.

Francesca had inherited the shop with her brother Michael from their recently departed father. They worked in shifts, one restoring while the other conducted business outside the shop and vice-versa. The layout was typical of Venecia; the workshop was in the back, the cluttered showroom was in the front facing the street.

Leaning up against a wall was an average sized, unframed canvas, maybe 100 years old, depicting Jesus and John the Baptist having their big day on the river. I picked it up and carefully set it on an armchair to get a better view.

"This is a good piece, yes?" Francesca said as she walked back to me taking her apron off. She was the picture of a statuesque Tiscian blonde, with a confident nose and chin.

"Yes," I agreed. "It is unusual to me; I can't tell who is Jesus and who is John."

"My guess would be him," she said pointing to the figure most in the foreground.

"Mine too, at first… but the other one's halo is bigger."

"Yes, yes. I see what you say."

"What are you asking for it?" I asked.

"One and a half million lire," she responded without hesitation.

"It is a fair asking price to start with," I pretended, trying to calculate, "but I am not in a position to buy anything today. What about the piano over there?"

"That is not for sale; it belongs to the family," she stated firmly.

"Is it any condition to play?"

"Of course. You are welcome to see, if we can make room."

"That would be nice. I have been missing to play."

"Prego, prego," Francesca said, and immediately began rearranging the corner of the room where the piano sat.

"I would like to hear the rest of the record first, if you don't mind," I mentioned as the piano was cleared.

"Yes, yes, I understand," she said. "This is good… I will return to my work in the shop, and you make yourself at home here, yes?"

"Yes, yes," I said. "Grazie."

"Prego, I will make espresso, si?"

"Prego," I said. "Grazie."

"Prego," she said in turn as she walked towards the back, getting the last prego in on me. This was typical of my last few days in Venice: I would ask someone for a cigarette and they would give me the pack.

I had arrived via the overnight train from Budapest, where I had spent two days at the Turkish baths and visiting the ancient Citadel. It had been a short but worthwhile stopover. I had placed a Urantia Book at the National Library and finished The Glass Bead Game in the kitchen of the Museum Hostel. The ending was abrupt. The Magister had finally achieved a comfortable level of self-realization, yet Hesse found no time for him to enjoy it. And just when I thought I had the book figured out. Bravo! My personal epilogue of the city proved almost as surprising.

I had already boarded the train for Venice and was leaning out of

The Drunken Tourist

the window of my compartment when I noticed a young man with thick glasses on walking back and forth on the platform with a package in his hand, apparently looking for someone on board the train. For some reason, he irritated me enough that when he passed by me for the third time I questioned him.

"Excuse me," I said rudely. "What are you looking for?"

"I am," he stammered, "looking for guest from hostel."

This surprised me, but it still didn't register. He continued, "Are you Santana?"

"Where are you from?" I asked, suspiciously.

"From Museum Hostel – I have something for Mr. Santana."

"Well," I said wondering how bad could it be (I had paid my bill), "that's me, I'm Santana."

He smiled and handed me a plastic bag with my torn, ripped up copy of Magister Ludi inside. I had left it on the kitchen table after sharing quotes with Eva, my host. She had sent this kid running clear across town to catch me before my train pulled out. This was my perfect epilogue of Eastern Europe.

If not for the recent past in Prague and Krakow and the future prospect of Venice, Budapest would have been a great place to get to know. The statue at the top of the citadel was the grandest I found in all of Europe and the prices were as cheap as Krakow. Yet at this point it was a stopover – I was anxious to get to the place I always dreamed of going, with two weeks to spare before my scheduled return to the States.

* * *

From the moment I stepped off of the train in Venecia, everything was in a swell of animated motion. This place was like no other – not even close. The spell of the place transfixed my unfocused glaze so powerfully that even the thousands upon thousands of tourists might as well have been added to the local pigeon overpopulation.

The waterbus dropped a throng of us off at the foot of a bridge, from where I proceeded to stumble up the steps, then stumble down without loitering. What did I know of the Rialto Bridge and the Grand Canal? I was on another planet – just find me a place to stash my bags so I could stumble around a little lighter.

Santana

I located the third hostel I tried after passing it twice. A business card was tacked next to a bell outside the enormous door, opening the walled entrance into a garden area, leading towards another door to the ground floor lobby. Through the lobby and up the stairs, past a third door, I was finally greeted by the "front desk" clerk, who led me to the last available bunk in a room of maybe thirty beds. Prego. They were booked for the rest of the week and the cost for the night was more than thirty dollars. Not so Prego. He gave me three keys; one for the first door, one for the last door, and one for the ground floor luggage closet. There was also a bathroom with a shower next to the closet.

A few thousand lire later, I walked out of there hands free, straight to the hardware store to have two keys made; one for the outside door and one for the luggage closet. I figured if worst came to worst, I could leave my big bag in the closet room for a while after I returned their keys. As it turned out, I ended up sleeping quite comfortably in the luggage closet the following evening. The space might have served me for a week or so, but Venice proved way too kind for all that.

* * *

During twilight time of the second evening, when everything was readily turning that fishtank green, I was sitting against a cement dock by the canal near the square of the Church of Santa Maria Formosa. Presently, a produce delivery boat pulled up and tied on alongside me. Two young men started to unload a couple of crates of bananas.

"Hey, give it here," I offered, motioning to the crate ready to be hoisted ashore.

"Prego, grazie," one of the fellows shouted as he lifted the bananas.

"And again," I declared.

"Prego, and again," he mimicked back.

"You speak English?" I asked.

"No, no," he said, "just a little; you speak Italiano?"

"No, no; no speak Italiano. What's your name?"

"Ricardo, my name is Ricardo," he said slowly. "And you?"

"Hadriano," using my middle name for the first time in years.

The Drunken Tourist

"My name is Hadriano – this is how you say, yes?"

"Yes, Hadriano," he said excitedly, "this is your town, you know."

"I know, I know," I answered, hardly knowing. The boat's engine was still purring, ready to ramble on in a moment.

"Hey, can I ride with you?" I wondered aloud.

They laughed a little at each other. "You are Americano, yes?"

"Yes," I answered, "I am Americano."

"You Americanos take the gondola, yes?" He sounded slightly sarcastic.

"I can't take a gondola," I answered, hands motioning empty, "I have no woman today."

They liked that one enough to put out a hand for me to climb aboard. Their negotiation of the boat through the narrow canals of the Rio del Plombo was masterful. Every time I thought they might hit another boat or a cement corner, the bumpers smoothed an inch away. We went a while with only the sound of the motor and Nicolo, Ricardo's best bud and partner, motioning towards landmark buildings and other boats along the way with approving gestures. They finally pulled up alongside a dock after a tight turn. Figuring the ride was complete, I stood up and grabbed my day bag.

"Hadriano, are you gone now?" asked Nicolo.

"I don't know," I stammered. "Can I stay on?"

"Of course," said Ricardo, "you stay with us; we only stop here."

Nicolo beeped the horn a few times, while Ricardo jumped off to tie up the boat. A minute went by before Nicolo's girl appeared, all smiles, with grocery bags in hand. She hopped deftly aboard, kissing both Ricardo and myself, and we were off again. One stop later and Ricardo's girl would be aboard along with another fellow whose name was never clear to me. One more turn after that and we were cruising on the highway of the Grand Canal. The wine then surfaced from the girls' shopping bags, along with the hash rolled and passed around Italian style (very slowly, with much waste). Battalions of Gondolas passed by with a casual salute, a taxi and a fishing boat pulled alongside us for quick conversations. The rhythm was everything. This was Sunset Boulevard and Broadway slowing down together in grand Venetian style. And what an eternal scene it was, with the green of Venice in all the light that was left.

Santana

Next stop was an outdoor restaurant, serving only the best pizza this side of Stromboli's, NY, and only to the local Venetians. Our table of six soon became a table of eight and then ten. When the pies were served everyone was surprised when I made bold to ask for a short prayer: "Bless us our Lord in these thy gifts, which we are about to receive from thy bounty. Through Christ our lord, Amen."

Approving Christos and Amens followed before we dug in. During dinner, we were joined by another Ricardo, a well dressed fellow my age who sat down at the other end of the table, talking to Ricardo and Nicolo, but concentrating on Nicolo's girlfriend the whole time. You could see how pissed off Nicolo was getting, but he kept his peace – this new Ricardo guy was obviously some local hot shot that commanded this kind of indulgence.

"Hadriano," he called to me from down the table, "do you know you have a twin in this town?"

"No, Ricardo, this is news to me," I replied. "Might I meet him?"

"He comes to my club every weekend, you can come too. I hear you are a piano player, Hadriano?"

"Yes, yes, I play a little but I have not found any place to even listen. Do you know where I can find any music?"

"Aye, you have noticed how quiet our town can get, yes?"

"Yes, I have noticed this… the sun goes down and everything disappears."

"Yes, this is true," he said. "Love is always better, but if you like, we will find you a place to play."

He handed me his card across the table, with everyone looking well pleased with the conversation. "Come to the club as my guest, of course."

"Ricardo, thank you," I said, "but first you must do me one favor."

"Yes, Hadriano, what can I do?"

"Nicolo is my friend," I continued, "and it would be difficult to be your guest while you pay so much attention to his woman. I'm sure you did not know this, but she is with Nicolo, who is your friend, I'm sure. In New York this would be very difficult."

Nobody said anything. He knew who she was, and everybody knew that he knew, but he had been all over her anyway.

"You," he proclaimed, "you are, how do you say in New York – you are crazy Modafuckeh."

The Drunken Tourist

"That's how we say it," I stated clearly and raised my glass. "Salute, Ricardo."

"Salute, New York," Ricardo smiled back.

"Prego!" The grin that came to Nicolo was priceless.

Whatayagonnado? These folks had no clue how many times my "buds" back home had left it to me to break the ice, only to dive into the icy waters of young ladies who loved to flirt. Nicolo's girl was clean on this one, but still, watching from the other end of the table got me boiling over my unfaithful ex. More wine was definitely in order and Fragolino would be just the ticket – the seasonal bubbly, strawberry wine in white and red, served chilled. It went down to hit me like champagne, but settled in like a good red. Soon enough, the Fragolino, the hash, the colors and the bravado of the evening had me quite high and back on the boat with our merry little band, cruising the Grand Canal for another burn down the strip.

Ricardo's driving was still steady as we took a turn down Rio Apostoli dei Gesuitti, parking it across from an ancient cemetery. The crew clamored out into a square, and proceeded immediately to light up again. I had had enough of the hash, but the drink was still with me. The café on the far side of the square was still open, so I walked on and ordered Grappa at a table within shouting distance of the crew. Nicolo soon came to join me with a new face along: Umberto. Smiling Umberto joined me at the table, hitting on the waitress in excellent English and then in Italian – presumably for my benefit. Once he ordered, he promptly stated his business; "Hadriano, I want you to know that I have been told you put Ricardo in his place tonight, and for this I am at your service."

"I am in need of nothing, sir," I answered. "As you can see, I am completely stoned and in good company."

"Yes, it is clear that you are very stoned," he continued, "but I am right behind you, and maybe I can be of help to you sometime."

"Salute, Umberto. Prego," I said, lifting my glass.

"Salute, Hadriano."

Apparently resentments run deep in old Venecia. Umberto related to me the tale of his long standing feud with Ricardo, something to do with a painting never returned or payed for. We spent the rest of

Santana

the evening getting to be paisans while hitting on every girl in the bar with no luck at all. The next morning he met me outside the luggage closet and carried my bags to his apartment. I was now the guest of honor in his home for as long as I wanted. Among other conveniences, Francesca's restoration shop was right around the corner.

For lack of a better term, Umberto made a living as an assistant magician for a number of local artisans. He had that unique quality of coordinating all the necessary materials for a great day and great work. Without asking, he went right ahead and attempted the same for me.

For the next few days while Umberto was out working, I attempted to paint under the influence of Fragolino and Marijuana. Inevitably, a masterpiece of mine from early in the day would be a good source of hilarity by the time he got home. In between bouts of genius, I would patronize the neighborhood bars as the drunken tourist with paint all over him, then later in the day I would clean up a bit to roam through the more well worn parts of town with the rest of the pigeons. If the timing was right, I would end up with a pint in the pocket, ordering a five dollar Coke at a table outside the bar in San Marcos Square, transfixed with the twilight while listening to the house band doing an exceptional instrumental of Sting's "An Englishman in New York." Five bucks was a steal for all this action.

The fact that those five bucks were my last five bucks was a small oversight on my part. I had been living on the mad money from the Mallorca boat ride thinking I had maybe $150 left in my account. Apparently I had less than $20. The phone number on my bank card only had the 800 number for the States, so I couldn't even call them to confirm my poverty.

Thankfully, I had spent the last few days being completely irresponsible with the last of my lire to the benefit of Umberto and friends, so when I broke the news to him, he took it well. Still, he was trying to scrape together his own mortgage for the month. We set about in earnest trying to find me a gig.

Umberto called his ex, whose current boyfriend played the clarinet. I could tell how difficult this call was for him to make, but that was the kind of guy Umberto was. I dug up Ricardo's number, who was happy to hear from me and said he would make a few calls. By

The Drunken Tourist

the end of the night we had made plans to meet them both the following evening at a restaurant near the Arsenal, a perfectly amazing, perfectly preserved fortress not far from Umberto's place.

In the meantime, an iron really can work wonders. A matter of lire was a matter of lire, and this city of mine was way too splendid to let all those zeroes get in the way. I figured Venice would be tits compared to being broke in Manhattan. Rule number one when the pockets were empty had always been to dress my best. The blue suit was clean enough and Umberto had plenty of ties to consider while I pressed everything before I hit the streets, cleanshaven.

"Bon Giorno, Hadriano," Concella greeted me from behind her bar facing out onto the square. "Fragolino already! Matu se patso! (you are crazy)."

"Bon Giorno, Concella. No Fragolino today; no lire today," I replied with my hands doing most of the talking.

"Hadriano, uno momento," she said motioning me to wait while she made me a plate of her baby shrimp and mayonnaise sandwiches with the crusts cut off. The protein went straight to my face in a flush – Grazie, Concella.

Next stop was Francesca's shop. By now she was used to me coming over and playing in the mornings. During my improvisations she would shout approvingly from the shop in the back, then occasionally come over and put her hands on my shoulders. Looking up, straight back without turning, my hair would nestle in her bosom while my eyes glazed past her cleavage towards her face looking down just out of kissing distance. She smelled of cilantro and turpentine. Another shot at love, out of reach on account of the drink. Could I rally in the noblest city in the world, stirred by this diversified diva? Hell no. By now I was far too gone and she was far too cool not to notice. She might have entertained the notion of restoring me if she hadn't seen me such a wreck right out of the box. Instead, we played it more like I was a stray pup coming by to please for a few morsels of affection.

Sobering up was not under present consideration – I had already told myself that back in the States would be the time and place for all that. Besides, I liked it here on this latest bender. I had never found a more conducive town in which to drink, everything lapping up against everything else in little waves – the crowds, the pigeons, the water against the cement, the thousands of tiny golden tiles placed one by one to form the masterwork in motion. The more I drank, the more I swelled with the impressionism of Venice. The rhythm was colorific and the rhythm was right for a chilled cup of white, an espresso with anisette, along with one, maybe two of Umberto's Dexadrine to start my walk towards a day where I'm moving just fast enough to not to be bothered or bored. And yes, all is romance and yes, anything can happen.

Along my way, there were no internet cafés or yuppie sports bars to find or to avoid. Neither did I find or look for any Katherine Hepburns on holiday. I had long since given up the pastime of asking directions (for the purpose of asking directions or not), and there was no particular political agendas on calendar, nor was there any music "scene." In the majority of situations, my sense of urgency and need for resolutions, when tempered accordingly, seemed to work well enough in contrast to the primary concern of the European attitude epitomized here in Venecia: the quality of the day being most sacred.

The prevailing spirituality of the community was so well exemplified in the masterworks, that it only made sense for the personal practice of any attempted communion with God to be quiet and understated. It seemed the city was mostly obsessed with enhancing the beauty that surrounded them, and the citizens, young and old, were content in their primary purpose – being Venetians.

Along with the bring your own bottle stores selling wine out of the barrel, the various depictions of non-suffering Christs around the city became my landmarks. The stroll across the Ponte del Academia, through the modern art at the Peggy Guggenheim, to the cathedral towards the tip of the city's tongue at Santa Maria de la Salute was my favorite trail of the old and the new saluting the everpresent.

Day or night, always the water would be the beginning and the end. When it was late, the black streets were almost cozy. Silence demanded respect, making steps light. Melody lines sustained. Wet deadends that served as U-turns gave the grateful bridges a better life.

This morning we were off to the island of Murano shopping for chandeliers. My lack of lire and need for drink proved not to be a concern. Everyone was so happy to see Francesca! She was glowing

The Drunken Tourist

like she was still being cooked in one of the workshop's kilns. The dressed up drunk with the semi-permeable shades on only added to her mystique and another glass to the table. Within a minute at every shop we went there would be treats and wine for both of us. Francesca would conduct her business while I, at a respectful distance, with my back against the mountains of colored broken glass shining in the sun, watched the master and the apprentice taming the animal glass at the ovens. One touch, one poke and the adolescent bulbs would swerve in fresh color and shape. Seemingly random turns and then another in the other direction would form the sperm globes that could barely hold their own in the heat, just long enough to surge for resurrection, only to die once more and blossom yet again, stronger this time, now ready to chill with a hiss in the wooden water barrels. The modest smiles of a workingman's satisfaction would follow.

By the time Francesca and I arrived at the restaurant in the square by the Arsenal, Umberto, Ricardo and Enrico (the clarinet boyfriend) had already ordered and were drinking with two Italian beauties. Francesca just oozed with credibility for me. We pulled up two seats and I "scuzie'd" myself to talk briefly with Umberto.

"You are amazing, you know that, Umberto?" I said.

"What do you talk about like this," he answered with that grin.

"You know, you sly dog," I continued. "You sitting here with these two enemies of yours, looking out for me like this; you're fucking beautiful, you know what I'm saying?"

"All I can say, Hadriano, is that you better be good on the piano, or else I am going to be shit. You can play, yes?"

"Fuck you, Umberto," I said, laughing. "Let's hope the little mouse boy over there can blow a little bit too, O.K.? What I want to see is this girl who used to be with you, who is now with him. Looking at him makes me wonder if there really is a girl at all. Tell me the truth Umberto, c'mon now, there is no girl is there? It's been Ricardo all along. You and him are secret lovers, yes?"

"Fuck you, Hadriano, fuck you," Umberto laughed. "You are my bitch now and you better be able to play."

"I will try to remember something for you," I said in earnest, "just to spare you the embarrassment, O.K.?"

"O.K. then, prego. Just don't drink too much, O.K.?"

Santana

"O.K. then, prego," I said walking back to the entourage, getting the last prego in on him.

Mouse-boy could blow after all. In fact, I never played with anyone so convenient. Then again, I never played with a clarinet player before either. For every change, he would find a turn. By second verses he could anticipate the chords, even the pauses. Mouse-girl was mesmerized and Umberto and Ricardo were noticeably proud of their production.

The piano was a shiny, black grand centered in the middle of the Pizzeria with long wooden self service tables fanning out on three sides of the platform that elevated about six inches from the floor. We stretched out our songs four or five times before switching keys for another.

There were long sections where we played modestly like background musicians at a cocktail party until we called the attention of the crowd with crescendos toward climaxes coming but not spent. We got bolder as the night went on and by the end of the second set I ventured a vocal while beats were slapped by a few enthusiasts at the wooden tables surrounding us.

Ends up, we pretty much nailed it. Mouse-man held one note at the end forever. I could care less that most of the audience couldn't understand half the words. The same could hold true at any gig in the States. Satisfaction had nodded my way for a minute and that minute was splendid.

As it turned out, this would be my first and last musical performance in Venecia. New York and then home to unresolved situations with Alex and my Queen were too much to seriously consider staying on. Considering the events that would soon come to pass, if there ever was an opportune time and place to relocate, this would have been it. Then again, in retrospect, who isn't a star?

Two days later, while Umberto distracted the ticket taker, I hopped the ferry to the airport on schedule, bound for New York. I had 1200 lire in my pocket (about a dollar).

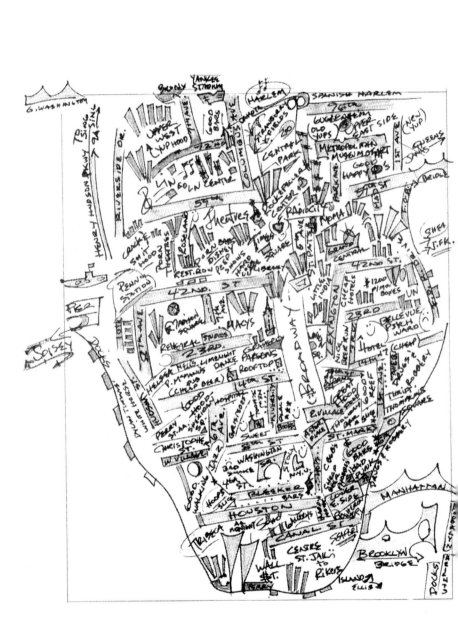

New York

Whatayagonnado? For the past few months I had not gone one day without a good meal and a good bed in places I had never been with people I could barely complete a sentence with. Now, back in my home town, I had just spent the last half an hour looking for a pay phone to spend the last bit of change I had in an unsuccessful attempt to find a place to stay for the night. The familiar dialing procedure had been the actual highlight of the calls.

John was my first choice. He was a good old bud that would put me up anytime without notice in his glorious top floor, floor-through photography studio. It was the kind of place you see in Woody Allen movies featuring struggling artists in New York that no struggling artist in New York could ever afford. There was no answer by four rings, so I hung up to spare the change. I tried my sister next - the generic message surprised me after two rings. Then there was Martha in Brooklyn from the train trip – phone disconnected. Chuck was next, up the Hudson an hour by train, but still a good friend with a nice house in the woods – again the machine. Stevie T's wife would never have me in on the fly so I didn't even bother calling him. Besides, Steven and I hadn't really had a good conversation in years. We both knew we had blown our shot at a music career together and there is no easy reconcile for all that. My Queen in L.A. was supposed to be the comfort call collect. She was home alright, now singing a different tune in a relative minor. As far as I was concerned, I would have stayed right there and taken the next flight to L.A. if she wanted me to, but as usual, she was playing it cold for no stated reason.

Santana

"Stay in New York; visit your friends and family," was all I got out of her. And this was after I told her that my friends and family were not around. Maybe I should have been grateful she accepted the charges for the call. Yeah right. The exhaust I got to suck outside the terminal waiting for the free bus to the subway was sublime compared to that horseshit I had just inhaled over the phone.

* * *

The thrill of being back in the greatest town on earth didn't fail to hit me, regardless. First stop in Manhattan was my sister's building on 12th and 6th Avenue. I thought I could get a spare key from the front desk and crash in her place. No such luck. The doorman did remember me, but he couldn't find a key, so I had to settle with stashing my big bag in a closet and keeping my valuables with him locked in the same drawer where the spare key was supposed to be. Aaaaye, tough guy, thanks for everything. Another call to John's studio on the way downtown ate the last of my change.

So what else was new? I was broke and spent on the streets of downtown New York... but hold on a minute, if Jana was still working the bar upstairs at the Boston Comedy Club or downstairs at the Baggott Inn, she could bail me out – just like old times. Sure enough, Jana was busy behind the bar when I walked in. She did a triple-take on my raggedy ass, saying something like, "I figured you were dead, Santana, and by the looks of you I wasn't all wrong." Nice to see you too, I responded in kind, "I see you've been moving up in the world. You being on the second floor and all." It was useless to explain to her the new twist on my all too familiar situation. She had heard all the variations before. She let out a long sigh and poured me a generous Jack Daniels on the rocks. It was good to hear a little American again.

Downstairs some band was revving it up, and no shit, as I went down to check them out, Stevie T was walking out of the bar with his guitar over his shoulder, fresh from a gig. He looked great. Stevie had always lived a charmed life, and it showed. Women took care of him, he just had it like that. Many drinks were certainly in order for this improbable reunion. Steve must have been doing well; he had at least

The Drunken Tourist

eight dollars to spend. Myself on the other hand, had the dummy debit card to forget at the bar after we ran up the tab to who knows what.

We didn't have to discuss anything. It just felt good to be next to each other again. My sister Elisa was the only person brought up from the past. She had been our biggest fan and spiritual support way back then. These days she wasn't interested in seeing either of us. Elisa was the most giving angel in the world until she lost it. And when she did, she really lost it.

But that was another story and tonight it was much like old times. We got hammered waiting for Jana to show, which she finally did – well coked up with more to spare. She was always good like that. Timewarp high ensued. The scene on the streets of New York were still the best in the world, walking Stevie back home to the East Village before Jana and I took the subway to Queens to meet up with Andy at their place. How Jana figured that her current boyfriend wouldn't mind me spending the night on their couch, I'll never know. This guy was mad. Plain angry. A real bitch weighing in at a fit 225 maybe 250, storming in and out of the door all coked-up, ready to blow me away any minute. Poor Jana. She was too good for this guy. Then again, she was too good for me, too. The best I could do was just get the hell out of there. Coming down off coke at six in the morning, broke in Queens, with no place to crash and not even a pair of shades on ? Lovely. After being back in New York for a matter of hours, I had reverted to the worst of it from ten years ago. I was a wreck in regret, trying to get out of Astoria as the city started to shine from across the 59th Street Bridge. The clear priority here was a pair of sunglasses.

The shades of the day were found on my fourth try at a diner that I hit on the way back downtown. "Hi, how are you… I know this is a long shot, but did you find a pair of sunglasses left here?" I asked the register guy, without actually lying.

"I don't know… what do they look like?" he questioned.

"They're sort of black, you know, sort of regular… thank you for looking." He shuffled through some junk drawer near the register. Eventually a pair did surface.

"Could these be them?" he asked holding up a dirty pair. "These look like they've been here for awhile though."

Santana

"Hey," I got a little excited, "I think those are them – could I see, please? Yeah, these are them," I said, again not lying. "These are just the shades I was looking for, thanks a lot."

Further distanced from reality, I bumbled down Lexington Avenue, a native son returning home as a juvenile delinquent way past his prime. Just like in Barcelona, instead of cutting my losses for the day, I felt compelled to embrace this dumb little run with a vengeance.

On the corner of 23rd, the supermarket was already busy by the time I selected my shopping cart and passed a check-out island to grab paper and plastic before I shopped. Milk, juice, cheese, bread, wine, cold cuts and cookies were all selected and placed in the baby seat before I got behind a mountain of oranges to fix paper in plastic in the body of the cart. First the milk and juice in the bottom of the bag then the rest was quick work before I rolled out through a vacant check out aisle, another satisfied customer.

With groceries in hand, I walked in through the out door of the New York Health and Racquet Club down by University and 13th. Stuffing everything in a locker, I grabbed a towel and headed straight for the sauna. They even had disposable shavers available at no extra charge.

The practice rooms on the 9th floor of NYU's Education Building had always been my number one reliable refuge in the city for the past fifteen years. It was right off the Southeast corner of Washington Square and the security guards must have figured I was a professor by now. In fifteen years, I might have been denied access twice. The 9th floor was entirely made up of small rooms with pianos, and one room would invariably be open. Just walking through the halls listening to the students practicing was rejuvenating. I found a room open, put a piece of paper over the little window, dragged the piano up against the door, ate and drank my fill, and crashed out on the floor for the next four hours.

If you dress the part, you can actually still have a pretty good day with no money in NYC. Of course it helps if you've already paid to advertise in a lime green Yankee cap with DKNY shades on, a Tommy Hilfiger T-Shirt, Calvin Klein briefs under your Speedos, Anne Klein cologne over everything, complete with a pair of Airs and the private label, limited edition, autographed socks from Ralph

The Drunken Tourist

Lauren. Don't you dare forget the Gap bag in one hand and your own Starbucks mug in the other or you're just plain off the rack. Now, how could any God-loving retailer resist rallying around your temporary fall from the graces of active consumerism?

Free coffee is a given considering your interest in sampling the slightly citrus medley of the day. The corner fruit venders and bagel carts always have something they're going to toss, and the line "Can you spare me a slice?" at any corner pizza joint can work or not work with minimal embarrassment.

By the time you get uptown, you could develop a St. Tropez tan courtesy of sampling stations at Saks on your way through Central Park to the Metropolitan Museum of Art for a suggested donation (Yeah, I got your suggested donation right ova'ere, pally). If it's Wednesday evening, the Museum of Modern Art goes at the same rate. You know the drill in the cafeteria. Fill up before you hit Broadway for the second half of any number of enchanting engagements now gracing the stages of The Great White Way.

Drinks are a little bit harder to come by, but if you map it out right, you'll do fine. Grab a free paper and look for lists of Art openings and Poetry readings. After a few spritzers, you'll see the genius alright (Hey, I got your genius right ova'ere, tough guy). Restaurant openings and small theatre closings are good bets to serve hard liquor for obvious reasons.

Come happy hour, the nicer the place, the better chance you have of running up a tab. Anybody hip could figure out just by looking at you that you work at the hottest club in town, your woman just left you, and your partner with the cash hasn't showed up yet. If all else fails, just go somewhere else and ask the bartender to spare you a fucking drink already.

Of course, the logical progression after all this would be one of a hundred of those other happy hours available around town in the rooms of Alcoholics Anonymous. This wouldn't be the first meeting I've attended half in the bag. Small wonder the pitch was canned and the responses that followed were textbook: "Oh thank you, Reginald, for your share, you are such a shining example of how this program works." (Hey, I got your shining example right ova 'ere Mr. Supersober).

Santana

Yeah, I was in a foul mood all right, about as constitutionally incapable of being honest as I'd ever been. At any rate, Chapter Five from The Big Book of Alcoholics Anonymous was being read so the damage was done. On a good day, a bout between Truth vs. Everything Else was at least interesting, but this evening it just hurt. "What an order! I can't go through with it," was enough for me as we listened on. "Do not be discouraged. No one among us has been able to maintain anything like perfect adherence to these principles. We are not saints. The point is, that we are willing to grow along spiritual lines. The principles we have set down are guides to progress. We claim spiritual progress rather than spiritual perfection."

Yeah, O.K. I got the point, but there was no way I was ready to give up a shot at becoming a saint in the name of a little spiritual progress. The more pertinent news (or so I thought), was that this very Church on 11th and 5th was growing along some spiritual lines of its own, giving me access through the basement to a room full of pews in the dark. I curled up in my trench and asked God for sleep or not.

The contractor who woke me was a sweet fellow. He could have gone ballistic, but the suit must have thrown him off just enough to show a little mercy. There is no need to elaborate on what a mess I was walking out of there, down Broadway past Canal. I was way too old for all this shit, and certainly feeling it. I finally found John at his studio only for him to greet me with sad news.

His woman worked as a location scout for a production company. Three days ago she had returned from Cleveland after spending a few days looking for possibilities for an upcoming shoot. Apparently her quest had not been completed to her satisfaction, but time would not allow further research. While she was waiting at the airport in Cleveland, she had run into a friendly local who struck up a conversation as they smoked their cigarettes outside the terminal. The location business was mentioned, at which point he made mention of a few spots near the airport that he thought might serve her purposes. Now this fellow just happened to have a friend driving a gypsy cab that could take them to the aforementioned spots while still allowing time for her to make it back for her scheduled flight. Within minutes she was in the back seat of this station wagon headed out to the long term parking area.

The Drunken Tourist

John wouldn't elaborate much of the details that followed. He did infer, however, that she had got away without penetration. Somehow she got herself out of the vehicle and ran back to the airport. Instead of reporting the incident to the authorities, she took the flight back to New York. This was somewhat understandable. It had taken John a couple of days to get the story out of her and now his girl was up at his mom's house in Westchester, convalescing. Today he was tying up some loose ends at the studio and was off to Cleveland this evening for revenge. He invited me to go. All he had to go on was a fair composite of the two pieces of shit who had tried to rape her, and the description of the vehicle: an early seventies Ford Country Squire with wood paneling on the sides. John was confident that the car could be found.

"And then what?" I asked him. "What are you going to do to them if you find them?"

"I don't know," he said, "but I've got to do something. I called the police in Cleveland, and if they don't get a report within 72 hours, they don't do shit."

"Maybe you should let it go," I suggested. "What does your girl say?"

"She doesn't know I'm thinking about going," he stated firmly, continuing to pack.

"John," I said, "I understand, really, but you might end up in the middle of a very nasty situation."

"I'll worry about that later," he said. "I want to find them first; then we'll see what to do. I just need somebody to come along for the ride. My brother is in Minnesota or else he told me he would come. What do you think?"

"What do I think? I think I might do the same thing… I don't fuckin' know."

"Then you'll come with?" he asked without looking at me.

"I'd think about it," I said, "but I'm broke."

"Well, what else is new. If you don't drink too much I've got enough cash for both of us, and we'll share a room when we get there."

"I was going to go up to Croton to visit my dad's grave before I left town. Could we stop there?"

"I'll tell you what," John replied. "I've got to pick up the car in

New Rochelle anyway, so I'll pick you up in Croton and we'll head out from there."

"Can I borrow a couple of bucks for the train?" I asked.

"Sure," he said. "You want some coffee?"

The ride up the Hudson River Line from Grand Central was a flood of mixed emotions. The smell of the train set off so many memories of all those mornings catching the 6:20 to recover in the country after all-nighters in town. From across the river, the trees on the Palisades were peaking in the sun and soon enough the tracks rolled past Sing Sing towards the peninsula of Croton Point up ahead.

Taxis have their assigned spaces in the parking lot at Croton-Harmon. Walking down to the lot from the bridge over the platform, I saw Rob waiting his turn for passengers in his Lincoln Mark VI. It was my father's car. Not the same make and model, but the same car. We had sold it to him two years ago during the wholesale panic that ensued after my dad's sudden death. I waved, walked towards him, and before he could get out I motioned for him to pop the trunk.

"Hi Rob, how's the car running?" I asked nonchalantly.

"Car's fine, haven't had any major problems. How are you... you don't look too good."

"I'm O.K.," I sighed. "Been on the road a lot."

"Are you going to the house?"

"The house is sold. I'm going to The Bank of New York and then to the cemetery. Can you wait at the bank then drive me up there?"

"Yeah sure," he said. "Hop in."

Same smell. A bit dimmer, but the whole family was still there in the back seat with me.

After doing business with the same branch of The Bank of New York for the past forty years, they had found it prudent to freeze the majority of my father's travel agency account for two years until the ARC could take their sweet time in settling matters. The bank manager could have helped expedite the whole affair, but of course his allegiance to a loyal client had disappeared a few days after that client was buried down the street. You could really feel the warmth

The Drunken Tourist

in the room from the whole staff when I walked in to finally close out the accounts. None of it mattered anymore. Congratulations to all of you on another two years at the bank. Two years in the grave and the father was still giving to the floundering son.

The mound at the grave was down now, but the rocks I had placed in the form of a cross were still visible if you knew where to look. This was our mound. Just me and my dad's. Once the casket had been lowered on that beautiful day two years ago, I had sent everyone away. The cemeterian with his pet bulldozer and Trevisani, my childhood friend, were the only three left when the involuntary ritual began – one shovelfull at a time. Sobbing and sweating, jacket off then the shirt, picking out stones worth picking up and shoveling again, thinking about my grand old man. All the big plans, the attempts to please and overcompensate, tempers lost and reconciliation, the family trying to make it through a meal at the dining room table, and all the teary-eyed scenes at the airport when he finally broke down as we said goodbye, trying to compose us with consolation cash covertly pressed in my palm. All this and so much more I hadn't thought of forever passed through me until it registered as one good grief. Sobbing and shoveling was the only right action there and then. Like an Indian of the Universe exiled to suburbia, the instinct of the ages was still working.

The only thing real was that in this grief, I was sure. I was surer of myself than I had ever been. With complete conviction, I knew the grief was real, so I knew I was real. No doubt about it – I was undeniably real with gravity.

The fraudulent tone of the absurd thoughts that followed only nailed down this verdict. Thoughts that just pop out of nowhere. Stupid thoughts clamoring around my head. Thoughts about some idiot character on television or how much we could get for an old chair in the garage. In the middle of all this grief how could these stupid thoughts exist? I must be a real shit to be thinking like this. What was wrong with me? Then it was figured. Nothing was wrong with me. I wasn't a shit. It was the thoughts that were shit and it was the tone of the thoughts that exposed the fraud. Now they were done. Father, thank you. "Resist not evil" was guiding me through what not to claim and where not to go.

Santana

Trevisani returned with a gallon of water and the cemeterian dropped off a sack of grass seed. I picked seven stones out of the pile and pressed them into the dirt to make a cross that remarkably resembled my dad's figure. I sprinkled some water on the fresh dirt with two fingers over the whole at the end of the plastic jug. Fistfuls of grass seed were next, falling through my fingers. More water and private prayers.

Sitting next to that grave this afternoon, I listened to the kids get out of the grade school nearby. How strange it was that my dad went there. Soon enough, the kids had all gone home. All he ever wanted was a little peace and quiet. I wondered how many times the grass on the grave had been cut since I buried him. Again with the nonsense. His sacrifice of days was not forgotten.

Cleveland

After much discussion I had just about convinced John that the reason Triscuits cost so much more than other salted snacks was in the development of the wafer itself. Intricately woven whole wheat, I stressed, does not come cheap. He was thinking it was some kind of Nabisco conspiracy. I retorted his paranoia with Frito Lay evidence – straight from the crinkled empties off the floor in the back of our Chevy Citation. "Nabisco uses partially hydrogenated soybean oil, whereas your Frito Lay product, for example, contains one or more of the following oils: Corn, Cottonseed, or Sunflower Oil. Plus the Triscuit is whole wheat – imagine the painstaking craftsmanship involved in keeping the fucking wheat whole after all of those changes. Case closed; there is no conspiracy here."

"You see how easily you accept their story, you fool. It was probably in the mid-fifties when Triscuits came out and everyone was willing to pay back then because there was no competition. Nabisco knew that somebody would come out with a similar product in a couple of years at half the price, so what did they do? They went into competition with themselves with the introduction of the Wheat Thin, thus cornering the market on the wheat based salted snack. That one-two punch was just too much for anyone to challenge since." He did have a point.

"Could you pull over and pop the trunk already?" I asked.

"You finished that fucking six-pack already?" he exclaimed.

"No, of course not," I lied. "I just want to break up the Genesse's with a couple of Stroh's. Besides, I've got to piss bad… pull over will ya; there's nobody in back of you."

Santana

"You are a demanding bitch when you drink, you know that?" John said, half seriously, as he pulled the car off onto the shoulder.

We were in the middle of Pennsylvania somewhere, heading west on Route 80, and both local amber brews had been complementing the fall foliage beautifully for the last four or five hours. Days like this took me back to high school times, so I was sucking it up as best I could under the circumstances. The serious side of our escapade was still a few miles down the road.

* * *

As soon as we got into Cleveland, we went straight to the airport and started cruising the parking lots, looking for the green Country Squire with the wood panels on the sides. The short-term parking structure might have had seven floors. John drove and took one side as I looked on the other, up and down the aisles. Cleveland has got to have more station wagons per capita than anywhere else east of the Mississippi. There were a few green ones, but they were the wrong green and none of them had the paneling.

The long-term lot was huge and took almost an hour to peruse before we headed out to check into a hotel about three miles from the airport. The first thing I saw on the television in our room was the same Carl's Jr. commercial and the same Dodge truck commercial I remember being on every ten minutes the last time I tuned in (about six months ago). Fuck the TV, even if that Dodge tune is a catchy little number.

We were back at the airport in an hour and after another cruise through the short-term parking structure we settled into a space outside where we could see the main area for cars to pull up for departures and arrivals. All I could think was thank God we weren't at Kennedy. This was something John really needed to do, results or not. So we sat. And sat and sat. Then we cruised the parking structure a third time before we sat again. I really love airports but prefer the inside of the terminal if there is a choice. John allowed me a break to walk around inside to check for the guy. It was cool playing the sleuth at the airport. Especially at the bar with a bourbon. The only plan we had was if we found them we would follow them, and after that, who knew? John had accepted the fact that I wouldn't have a hand in any kind of violence.

The Drunken Tourist

Considering the shape I was in, my eyes on the lookout were my only real threat anyway. John, however, was extremely accomplished in the martial arts, so my own self-defense wasn't a real concern if things got dicey. Besides, the old Louisville Slugger lay waiting on the floor in the back under the salted snack food wrappers, just in case.

"Why don't we go into town and check out the bars and look for them there," I asked getting back in the car.

"What did you do, have a drink in there?"

"Yeah," I said. "I had a drink, but we could go to the bars in town and cruise the parking lots anyway. It's prime time Friday night, maybe they're out getting loaded or something, I don't know."

"Yeah, well, maybe," John replied. "Maybe we'll cruise the parking lots of the bars downtown or this Sin City strip the hotel lady told us about. First let's do another round in the parking structure."

"John," I said, "we would have seen them come in if they had gone up there."

"Listen bro, there's plenty of ways we could have missed them. We'll go one more time around, then circle back here and then go."

"Fine," I said. "Let's go one more time. But let's go straight to the top and then look on our way down this time, O.K.?"

"O.K. then," John sighed as he started up the car.

We got about ten feet into the short-term parking structure, right around the first turn before we were cut off by a car coming the other way. Close behind us was another vehicle that pulled up to our back bumper and stopped. Airport Security. Fuck. The big man in the car in front came out and walked over. "Both of you get out of your vehicle now!" John and I both hesitated. "Get out of the vehicle now!" the big man roared as he got to John's window. "O.K. you," he barked at John. "Shut the car off and take the keys out of the ignition."

Meanwhile, my door was being opened for me, courtesy of Big Man #2 coming up from the rear.

"O.K. you," he said to me calmly, "get out slow and put your hands on the hood." John and I stared at each other from across the roof. I noticed the car really needed a wash as Big Man #2 patted me down.

"O.K., don't either one of you move, stay right where you are," Big Man #1 barked. "Both of you." We weren't going anywhere, even though these guys smelled bad and their grammar was poor. Big Man #1 took John's keys from him and opened the trunk while #2 rummaged through the back seat. He emerged with the baseball bat. #1 slammed the trunk closed and waved off a car trying to get by.

"O.K., fellas," said #1. "What have you been doing here all day?"

John could take it from here. "We've been waiting for friends to come into town and we thought we might have missed them, so we were checking the parking lot for their car."

"What's with the bat?" asked #2.

"That's been in there for ages," I said. "We forgot to take it out before we left from New York."

"Let me see your license and registration," #1 asked John.

#2 continued, "You guys are from New York?" He must have noticed the plates. "What are you guys doing here?"

"Like he said," I replied, "we're meeting some friends here for the weekend."

"Yeah right," #2 said. "What do these 'friends' look like?"

"Well," I stammered, "one guy has sort of long blonde hair and wears glasses and the other guy is thin with short brown hair." Whoops, I had just pretty much described the two guys with their hands on the hood.

"You guys just stay where you are," barked #1. "We're going to run your plates." Maybe this sleuth business wasn't so cool after all.

"Well," the big man said to John, "your car checks out with your ID, so I have to assume you're not looking to steal a car today, so why don't you tell us what you're really doing here? Your partner over there is full of shit, so maybe you can tell us why you've been sitting at the airport all day before we call in a report to headquarters."

John then laid it down as best he could. After he had stumbled through most of it, #2 interrupted:

"Why haven't you gone to the police?"

"She didn't report it to the police. Like I said, she went right back to the gate and took the flight," John answered.

"What are you guys going to do if you actually find these guys?"

"I don't know exactly. We were going to follow them then maybe call the police."

"What were you going to say to the police, that you just found two guys in a station wagon that look like you? You guys are too fucking

The Drunken Tourist

stupid to make this shit up, so I want to believe you, but you can't come into town doing this and you certainly can't sit around here all day looking for this station wagon."

"Excuse me, sir," I asked, "but have you heard about this kind of shit going on around here before?" Turns out Cleveland had something like 80 sexual assaults or rapes reported a month. And those, they stressed, were only the ones reported. They recalled nothing of two guys who looked like us in an early seventies Country Squire with wood side paneling. And yes, they knew what kind of car that was. Big Man #1 had softened by this point, sympathizing a bit in his warnings, but still telling us politely to get the fuck out of the airport and go back to New York. We got out of there alright, headed back to New York via downtown Cleveland.

Whoever came up with the phrase "Cleveland Rocks" knew what the fuckin'A they were talkin' bout. We passed a shitload of jamming bars along the waterfront as we cruised the parking lots on foot. Small vessels were whooping it up along the waterways and the pedestrian traffic was similarly irreverent. Only one or two bars that we popped into were charging a cover and the beer was dirt cheap. Bands were playing filthy blues with plenty of young rockers actually dancing their asses off. Thankfully absent was the protocol moat formed in a semi-circle in front of the stage by the semi-timid who had already used up most of their self allotted dare for the evening in front of the mirror at home getting ready to go out. And although the safety headbob which had so insidiously infiltrated the American dance floor might have something to do with big hair, Cleveland apparently would not stand for it. Anyone on the dance floor who was not actually dancing was accordingly treated with no respect at all. This neighborhood was downright enchanting.

"Hey, we can dance well together, yes?" I yelled in the ear of some rocker girl dancing next to me. You bet I was suave, still moving a little, and still trying out that curious phrasing I had picked up overseas.

"Where are you from?" she asked, according to plan.

"Well," I said (here we go), "I'm from New York, but I've been living in L.A., and now I'm staying here. I really dig this city. Is it your hometown?" What a classic, bullshit line. It was full of barroom liberties without really lying – inferring infinite possibilities while giving a glimpse of my grandeur in a nonchalant way, making the glimpse so much grander and then finishing with the open ended question. God, I was so full of shit. No matter who, no matter where, if there was an opportunity to impress somebody, there I was trying.

"Your face is all red," was her response after all that. "Are you O.K.?"

"Yeah, I'm fine," I sighed, seizing the opportunity to add to my mystique and go for the sympathy vote at the same time. "I've been on the road a lot these days. You want a drink?" Again with the sales tool at the end.

"Well…" she hesitated, "sure. I'll have a Coors Light."

My love for her then faded. We had a beautiful thing going for a while, but I knew right then it was never going to work out. After all, how in the world could a beer be any lighter than a Coors in the first place? Now I had to suffer through with some dignity, waiting in line to order her flavored spring water while my partner was out looking for bad guys. "So you like Cleveland?" she asked, all cozy now that I wasn't all over her.

"So far, so good," I said, looking around. "I got here a few days ago with an old partner who needed help with some business he had to take care of."

"Oh," she said. "What kind of business are you in?"

I couldn't resist. "My partner's girlfriend got assaulted at the airport a week ago and now we're here looking for them."

"Oh," she said. "That's nice." There was a bit of a pregnant pause.

I was forced to go with my best line. "What?"

"It's nice that you're helping out your friend," she continued to cover herself. "Did you see the last band playing? The drummer's a friend of mine. The bass player is too, but the drummer is a real good friend." Well, there you go. Deep down, my gut instincts had told me all along that we weren't right for each other. What was important to me wasn't important to her. The children would have grown up very confused.

After checking out the following morning, John decided to go by both the bus station and the train station before we left town. We had

The Drunken Tourist

breakfast in the car and halfheartedly continued our search past the stadium then to the Amtrak station. Once we were there, I figured to check and see how far my train voucher could take me.

Originally, the special promotion was for a one way ticket straight from New York to any destination within the continental United States. Whether I could change the departure point, I had no idea. To Amtrak's credit, they would still honor the ticket from Cleveland to Chicago then on to Los Angeles, as long as my stopover in Chicago didn't exceed twelve hours. It took seven hours from Cleveland to Chicago and from there I could take the South West Chief for the forty-three hour ride all the way to L.A. And I could book the whole thing right there in Cleveland. The way the guy was taking care of me at the Amtrak ticket window, you'd figure he was working off commission or something.

It was due out in less than an hour. That didn't give me much time to think about carrying on from there or going back to N.Y. with John to catch a flight home in a day or so. What I was thinking about was the fifty hours of recovery time the train might afford me starting right there and then.

John understood a little too readily when I mentioned my options. It was a toss up figuring who was more eager for me to get on the train – the Amtrak guy or my buddy John. This was not the first time that the results of my tendency to burn through people had become clear. Even John had had enough of me in three days, after I hadn't seen him for years. In a minute I was alone in the train station, waiting for the Lake Shore Limited bound for Chicago.

From one of the pay phones closest to the platform, I called 911 two minutes before I got on board my train. The report was there were two guys in a green, early seventies model Ford Country Squire with the wood paneling on the side, one with blonde hair and glasses and the other one with short brown hair, who had just left the scene of a hit and run.

Los Angeles

I dove into her face. My beautiful baby! Intact, here, right here. Our hug buried me in her breasts where I could now finally rest. My Queen, my sweetheart, my Sweatheart and my everything for all intensive purposes needed me as much as I needed her. She was all over me, please stay all over me, still let's get closer. That center of my own individuality that I had found on the road was the first souvenir I would lay at her feet.

Next was every inch of me. We didn't even go back to my place. The closest motel was a few blocks away and we had all the supplies we needed. At first the lovemaking was almost careful. Inside my happy girl, pleasing my jewel, we had a long summer day on our island home. Then tight, together, we hitched upon a star and left the earth behind on a perfect breeze. Starting to sweat then smelling our sweat, leaning into each other harder and harder, we laid claim to another constellation as ours alone. Yes, we will own each other now.

Nothing came close to this. Our star was a Supernova. From under the covers she read me the most beautiful letter anyone has ever written me. She was going to take care of me and we were going to live a beautiful life togther. It filled up the hole that had been with me forever. We ordered in and she asked me how the train ride was and why it had taken so long. I told her just enough so it wouldn't make her feel like she really missed out on anything. Truth was, she really hadn't.

Straight from Cleveland the Amtrak employees had made it crystal clear what an honor and privilege it was to be riding on their train.

Santana

Not the conductor, but the big cheese ticket lady's ass was so large that when she stalked down the aisle she had to maneuver left then right to avoid hitting the seats. We arrived in Chicago two hours late and the connecting train I was booked on had already left. The next South West Chief scheduled to depart four hours later was booked solid. The best they could do was put me on standby for the following train which left four hours after that or else reserve me a seat on the train that left four hours after that one. The whole business was in chaos and all the agents were overwhelmed. Amtrak must have been running a hundred different specials with a hundred different contingencies. I ended up bitching to the right person long enough to get a sleeper share, provided the space stayed available.

I ended up sleeping for 8/10ths of the trip. Otherwise I was eating or playing Rummy 500 in the bar car with two fellows headed for Phoenix. There was about a hundred miles in New Mexico that was the only scenic part of the ride that I was able to catch, while the sleeper share for four was mine alone for the whole trip. The difference between Eurail and Amtrak had been night and day for me, but I wasn't going to get into all that with my beautiful baby looking up at me with those big eyes fixed on mine.

We were true lovers for the next few days. Off to the beach and then to the hills. Bowie's "Wild is the Wind" was everywhere. Then back into town to pick up my car and drop hers at the shop. I didn't even go home or call Alex. We stayed at the hotel and ate well, went shopping and danced like mad with our eyes only on each other. It seemed we transmitted our glow towards whoever we ran into. My ship had come in. There was some money now in my account due to a few agency refunds from the settled account back east and I wanted to spend a good bit of it on my Queen. Reality would have to wait a few more days. Then we could settle in, motivated towards the life she was talking about in that letter.

Day three came around and I went to my house to find it trashed. The nefarious slob I had sublet to hadn't even taken the garbage out since I had gone. It just laid there in bundles all over the property. Well fuck you, you shit, you're out. You'll get what's coming to you. Life was too good to freak. It was Monday night and I was going to get back on the

The Drunken Tourist

good foot while the getting was good. Besides, with all this love energy happening, I figured the withdrawals wouldn't be that bad this time around. My A.A. group on Monday night had seen me in and out so many times in the past five years it wasn't even embarrassing for me anymore to show up as a newcomer, again. Most everyone there was always glad I had made it back, and those that copped an attitude, well fuck 'em; life was too good to freak.

After the meeting, I called my baby just to check in. I knew she had work to do and I needed to finally get settled. She answered completely cold on me. A different girl. What could have changed that much in six hours I still don't know. She just shut me out. No reason. She didn't explain and she didn't want to make plans. She wanted to catch up with me in a few days, maybe, but now she had to go. What!? Trying to compose myself, I searched for my center and found it gone. The line was off the hook when I called back. Remaining calm was a fleeting notion as I got in my car and sped to her house. She was lying in bed when I opened her door.

"Hey," she startled, "you can't just come over like this."

"Your line was busy" I panted. "What happened to you? What's the matter?"

"Nothing's the matter." She started raising her voice, "you're just making a big deal out of nothing again. I want you to go, I need to be alone."

"What did I do?" I pleaded. "Is this how you treat anybody when nothing's the matter? Baby, I love you, you can tell me anything. Don't shut down on me, please. Don't shut down on us…"

"Listen to me," she interrupted, screaming. "You're smothering me again; I've got a life too, you know. I can't devote all my time to you, I've got finals coming up and I can't concentrate… now you have to leave me alone!"

"Baby I'm sorry… you know how insecure I can get. I would never shut you out like that on the phone. We just had three beautiful days together, and now this? Please don't do this."

"Well, I'm sorry" she stated in monotone. "If you can't handle it, we don't have to go on at all. This is all too much for me and I've got work to do. Do you understand me?"

"I know we can't go on with me and you completely crazy in love for three days then you go completely cold. I can't take it."

Santana

"I can't take this either," she was screaming again. "It's too much, you're too much, you're too demanding, you're driving me crazy, do you hear me? You have to go! You have to leave now, before it's too late!"

"Too late for what?" I yelled back. "Don't do this, baby, I love you, I don't want to leave like this."

"Listen to me! You can't come over here anytime you want – now go, get out! My landlord will hear us and he'll call the police."

"Let him call the fucking police; I don't give a shit. Now what the fuck is up?"

"Listen to me," again with the monotone, "you have made a big thing out of nothing, now get out of here, I will call you in a couple of days. You have to leave me alone! Get out of my house already, do you hear me?!"

I heard her alright. I was crushed. Went straight to the bar. Then to Pico and Hoover to buy a shitload of crack. Booohjaaahhh… what a hit. Now that would do me. Yeah right. Three or four hits later and it's all Red-Alert paranoia driving home by the rear view mirror. Walking into my own private disaster area, I spread out all the memorabilia I had collected from each city that I had visited on my trip in a circle around me. Magister Ludi and the Urantia Book in the center next to me with a bottle of some crap and the crack pipe loaded with the rest. Now what? Fuck it all. I called my old dealer to commit to the worst run of my life. He was over with a sack in an hour. Three days went by spent mostly at the window. The helicopters were dangerously close.

When she finally did call and come over it was too late. She went off on what an addict I was while I screamed whore. Then we fucked our way through all that was left of anything good. When I woke up she was gone.

Two days later I got myself together enough to try to visit Alex. The restraining order his mom had put out during the court battle months ago was still in effect, except for the court ordered visitation times. After three or four calls to their place with no response, I drove over to find my ex-wife sitting on the stone wall outside her apartment building. Without getting out of the car, I asked her

The Drunken Tourist

how she was. I let her know I was back for good and we agreed that we would start up visitation again at the allotted time. Alex was at a friend's, but he would be back soon. There was a parking space around the corner, so I decided to leave the car there and go to the nearby pizza joint to watch the game and wait for Alex.

Walking back to my car an hour later, I saw Alex in the alley in the back of his place, walking towards me with his mom's new man. I waved excitedly as he picked up his pace my way before the new dick held him back to let two police cars pass. They stopped three feet in front of me and got out of their vehicles.

"Mr. Santana, right," asked one of them, walking towards me.

"Yeah, that's me. What's up, officer?"

"Can I see some identification please?"

"Why, sure," I said. "What's happening here, anyway?"

"Just let us have your I.D.," another one chimed in.

Meanwhile, a third car pulled up. My ex had called the cops on me for violating the restraining order. Technically, I was less than a hundred yards away from her and technically all violations of restraining orders are domestic violence reports whether there is any domestic violence stated on the order or not. Mine was obviously not. The cops knew that. I had unsupervised visitation rights with my son right there in black and white. They didn't give a shit. And by the way, Mr. Santana, the tags on your vehicle are expired so we are towing your car while we tow your ass to jail.

Today was Friday so I would have to wait until Tuesday to see a judge. Everybody involved knew any judge would let me go on this bullshit, but they needed to teach me a lesson. They did give me a phone call which I used to call my Queen in exile, of all people. The answering machine got the message.

I passed Friday, Saturday and most of Sunday alone in a cell. Three quarters of the time was spent asleep or forcing myself back to sleep.

"I'm still in the game," I kept saying to myself. "All is not lost."

Sunday afternoon the intercom called me and the door was buzzed open. "Sure enough," I thought, "our love was too big to be denied. She's come around again." The officer of the day came through his door to greet me as I came through mine.

Santana

"Sign this," he said, as he served me with papers for a new restraining order which my Sweatheart had just filed. Boom. Just like that my heart collapsed. How could she?

Monday's holiday passed and Tuesday morning the judge let me go with time served and summary probation. I called Gordon to help me get my car out of hock to the tune of two hundred and something dollars, plus the fix-it tickets. He was one of the few friends I had left that would accept me drunk or sober, preferably sober, which I definitely was for a change.

The following days were a blur of melancholy, attempting to get my house together and weighing my options for the future. My mom was really the only voice of reason and support I had going. It's uncanny how in times of crisis nobody shows up. I had learned the definition of a "fair weather friend" when my dad passed and now, here I was again. And still I hadn't seen Alex.

Three scheduled visitation rendezvous then passed with no sign of him. Somewhere in between all this cleaning and agonizing and unpacking and all those fuck-its, I found a good size sack of crack that I somehow missed during previous crumbing debacles. There had been recent nights where I would hide the stuff in paranoia, only to search for it hours later. Today there was no hesitation in lighting up again. One hit later and it was all over. Looking back, without doing something positive to bolster the little bit of whatever momentum I had going from those days alone in the cell, it was just a matter of time before the inevitable breakdown. And this time I had left behind the ability to stop. There was no stopping for days. The freak was completely oppressive save for a split second of sucking in. And that was just in anticipation of nothing but exhales of Red-Alert at the window. No one was coming. And if they were, it was going to be really bad news. When my dealer wouldn't answer my call, I would have to get bold enough to venture out to the hood in Venice or downtown again or even somewhere close by to my house to find another crack addict willing to cop for me in exchange for a hit or two. Then I would wait and wait and wait, praying only that he would return.

If I got lucky and my man would come back, sometimes he would come to my house to smoke before he saw me high again. Then he would leave, suggesting I get some help. Inevitably, I would end up ly-

The Drunken Tourist

ing in bed with the sun already up, trying to force down some alcohol with the fleeting notion that my soul might be on trial. Curiously enough, my only source of comfort was in that notion. But instead of sticking with this brief bit of clarity, I would end up calling my fucking Sweatheart Queen. I was so far gone I guess I figured that if she came around, I would come around. Calling for hours and hours, getting the machine then leaving messages, then not leaving messages. Too fucked up to dare walk out the door too far away from the house. Besides, she could come to the window any minute now.

After my latest series of beggings, she finally agreed to come over, insisting that we were only going to the movies, and nothing was going to change. I'd take anything at this point.

"What would you say," she whispered to me in the back row of the packed theater, "if I told you that I slept with two guys since I've seen you?"

"I would ask you," I said carefully, "if they were anybody I knew."

"Well," she said, "you don't know them. One is my new neighbor and the other one was a guy I met at a club." My body sprung right out of the seat and through the door. She finished the film.

My fuck everything walk along Wilshire Boulevard was broken up by maybe five or six bars along the way. The next thing I remember, I was at the back door of my ex-wife's place.

"Oh my God," she said. "You startled me. What are you doing here? You know you're not supposed to be here."

"I'm sorry," I said, "I didn't know where else to go. I miss Alex so bad and I can't stop drinking again. I need some help. Could we sit together please, just for a minute, and then I'll go."

"You have to go now. Go now before Alex sees you like this."

"It's O.K., it's O.K.," I kept wailing, "I don't care, he'll understand. I just want to sit here with you for a minute."

"O.K., O.K.," she said calmly. "I'll make some tea and I'll call a practitioner from the church, O.K.?"

"O.K. that sounds good, thanks a lot," I said. "Where's Alex?"

"He's at a neighbor's house," she said from the kitchen. "Just relax, I'll be right out."

It was two or three minutes before she called me so I could get on the phone with the practitioner. I was open to listen and he was open to meet with me. I listened to his pitch while my ex-wife served me tea at the dining room table. When she opened the front door, there were two L.A.P.D. officers on their way up the path. This was not happening.

"Take your hands out of your pockets and put them over your head!" I looked at her and she turned away.

"Put your hands up! Now!" They met me outside the doorway and grabbed both my arms, swinging them in back of me as my face hit the ground. One jumped down on my butt and the other one grabbed one of my arms, pulling it further up my back. We struggled again until one of them sat on my back and started to cuff me. He jerked my arms still harder and I kicked out in pain. My boot smashed a fourth's cop knee before another one put all the weight he could across both my legs. I was done.

Bail was first set at $60,000. After my ex-wife and the arresting officers testified at the preliminary hearing, the judge raised the bail to $100,000 and the case was transferred to Superior Court in Santa Monica. Violation of Summary Probation, Violating the Restraining Order, Resisting Arrest and Battery on a Police Officer were the charges. The battery charge was a serious felony. My public defender was cringing. Like I said, I was done.

My last denial was my ex's betrayal. This denial attempted consolation but it didn't work. What happened to me, I did to myself. There was no way to bullshit out of this one. I was guilty. Nothing creative or original was going to change that. In fact, attempts in that direction only made me feel worse. I was an inmate now, scared shit, looking at real time. It was time to pay. For everything. For so long.

So this is fear. I'm shivering with my head under my stained blanket, having to piss but not daring to get up again because the guy below me had made it very clear that I was disturbing him when I got down off my bunk. I caught a terrible cold during processing and my mouth exploded with tooth pain a couple of hours after getting arrested. All I could do was try to find a place of comfort somewhere inside me but my guilt would not allow it. It was time to pay. My spit on life was now a flood of remorse soaking me in cold sweat stink. "God, I'm sorry," was pitiful. "Father, please let me sleep," was more realistic.

The Drunken Tourist

Processing is brutal. The new "fish" are those that come off the long bus ride from all over L.A. County to Central Jail. The handcuffed chain is herded into a 20' x 20' room. The cuffs are taken off at the door until there's sixty seven of us stinkers standing there. No one can sit and believe me, you have time to count. You also have time to smell every rotten fart or pissed pants or sockless shoe. There are no open windows, just the wire windows looking to Room #2. Everyone is nodding out or coming down, pissed off as hell. Eye contact is avoided at all costs. When the door to Room #2 finally slides open, the stink is worse. "Left shoulder against the wall!" barks the deputy, "bump it up gentlemen, bump it up!" My nose is brushing up against the afro in front of me. "O.K. now," the deputy continues shouting, "take everything out of your pockets, place it all on the floor, then put your left shoulder back against the wall. Now!"

Once done, two deputies rifle through the mess on the floor then start checking wristbands for entrance into Room #3. Waiting against the wall you can see what's going on in there. There is a female deputy in charge. "O.K. gentlemen, this can go easy or not. It's up to you. The faster we get this done, the sooner you can move on to your bunk. Now strip it down. You have thirty seconds to take off all of your clothes. Do not shake your socks. Lay them down easy. Let's go! You have thirty seconds." Fuck me. I still had my Dad's wedding ring on that doesn't come off and my Holy Spirit medallion around my neck.

"When your clothes are off, turn around and put your hands on the wall. Let's go gentlemen." Half a minute goes by. "Now take your hands off the wall and touch your toes." Another fifteen or twenty seconds go by. "O.K., now put your hands on your ass and spread your cheeks. Spread 'em wide, let's go!" At least thirty seconds go by in this position. What dreams these deputies must have. "O.K., pick up your clothes, you have thirty seconds, then put your shoulder back up against the wall. Let's go! Bump it up!"

Through the next door wristbands are scanned and you are allotted a room with long metal benches to wait on. There is a metal toilet with no seat in the corner. The wait in this room for your name to be called is two hours, at least. "Santana, window twelve," finally.

Behind window twelve sits a considerate looking lady. "Last three"

Santana

(the last three numbers of your booking number). "Let me see your wristband," she goes without looking up. "Date of birth. Thoughts or plans of suicide?" Next question, "are you a member of a gang?" Finally, "are you allergic to any medication?" "Fingerprints, window twelve," she intercoms. A deputy comes by to do the dirty deed again. Then back to the same room with a little green card in my hand with my name and booking number on it. Water. Room on the bench. The television above us is on. I Love Lucy.

A group of names are called and we file into one of the three small rooms next to a large room with maybe ten rows of long metal benches. We are packed in there for an hour, maybe two hours, maybe two and a half hours, I don't know. Somehow I was able to find a space on the floor. Somebody kicked me when my name was called. Santana is a good jail name. The Eses (the Hispanics) want to respect the Wood (as in peckerwood, as in a white guy) with that name. One black plastic bag was given to everybody called out from the three rooms.

"O.K., gentlemen, put your green card in your plastic bag." Done.

"Now you have thirty seconds to take off all your clothes and put them in your plastic bag. Let's go!" Now we're naked and forced to sit with our legs spread apart on these cold metal benches. "Bump it up!" My chest against someone's back and someone's chest against mine. Their ass against my groin. The smell. Fuck, the smell everywhere. Forever minutes and we're all naked rubbing against each other. Fuck. "O.K. gentlemen, pick up your bags and file out of here."

In the next room throw your bags in the containers and pick up your bundles. Now move it! Hey you! You asshole, I said move it!" The inhumanity of the deputies was mesmerizing. They used to spray you down with a big hose before the showers with some anti-lice shit, but today it was directly into the showers. 60% Hispanic, 30% Black, and 10% Wood. I saw two guys that looked like they were from the Middle East and one Asian guy.

Collectively refreshed and comparatively natty, we donned our out-sized County blues, a white tee shirt and socks, then waited for our County shoes in a room that must have housed about two hundred of

The Drunken Tourist

us. "O.K., gentlemen," went the intercom, "lay out, it's going to be a while." They had us all sleeping on the floor trying to come down and deal with the fact that we all had just got busted. How I fucked up! Again!

By day four or five I was transferred to 2200 Cell Block B. 12 cells in a row, all of them 12x12x12. Three double bunk beds in each. A sink and a metal toilet in the corner. Every cell was full. Matt was across from me on his top bunk. He was in for a quarter gram of speed found under his accelerator pedal when he got pulled over for expired registration tags. He was waiting to see if he was eligible for the house arrest program, an electronic monitoring program for non-violent crimes.

Rodney, a 21-year-old gospel rapper was in for a "petty with a prior." He was looking at eighteen months. Ernie, the most ador-ably round little fella was in the bunk under Rodney. Ernesto was in for sales, looking at two years. He was always joking and trying to get an extra cookie or two from the trustees coming by with lunch. We got out of the cell twice a day for breakfast and dinner down the hall.

That was it. One day a week we got to go on the roof for a couple of hours. Louis, who spoke virtually no English, just got busted for trying to sell a van full of about a thousand pairs of Levis. He was looking at formal probation. Go figure. Brian, a white Hollywood hoodlum was looking at ten to fifteen years for sales. How he kept his humor I have no fucking clue. We discussed at length and in great de-tail the procedures in the manufacturing of new identification papers and good speed. "Yes," Brian explained to me, "obviously you do have a drug problem. And the problem is you're not doing the right drugs. You're a white boy – white boys don't do crack; white boys do speed. Drug problem solved."

About a week into it, Matt bought coffee from the canteen and shared it with the whole cell. Brian got all hyped up and set a trap with a piece of baloney on a string as we all waited in hushed hilarity for a rat to come out. Ernie got called to court the next day. He left me his pencil and New Testament. I ripped out an empty page to write to my dear departed:

Santana

Dad,

I'm having a hard time right now. Seems the world has got no heart for me anymore. Have I used up all the tenderness given to me for life? When I dare to look outside this icebox I see two women that keep kicking, a son I can't get to, and a trail of wreckage that hurts to see. I thought I did better than that.

I know no one will ever treat me as good as you have, but anything right now would taste twice as sweet to this ungrateful son. Thanks for always being there for me, Dad. Our dreams have been wonderful lately, haven't they? I do wish you had had more friends over at the house. You deserved them. Mom's been good. You should be proud. I'm sorry about... you know. As well as the... you know. There's got to be a way to turn this around. Somehow we are a successful family. Love.

One afternoon, the cell got a hold of a Saturday's edition of the Los Angeles Times. On the second page of the Religion Section, I opened to a little picture of Paramahansa Yogananda. That picture had always been with me, ever since I read "Autobiography of a Yogi" at sixteen. In that portrait with his Mona Lisa mouth and sincere look, I could always tell how I was doing in the eyes of God. Today there was a hint of a smile. The lesson for this Sunday at The Self Realization Fellowship was "The Liberating Power of Affirmation."

In the Calendar Section was a review of Van Gogh's upcoming exhibition. The newspaper's representation of his last painting with the black crows in the field was the first bit of beauty I had seen in weeks. I tore it out and stuck it with toothpaste to the ceiling, above my bunk next to Paramahansa's picture.

In the Book Review Section, there was an article about a Portuguese poet I'd never heard of. Fernando Pessoa's "To be great, be whole," was everything to me in that cell:

> To be great, be whole; exclude
> Nothing, exaggerate nothing that is you
> Be whole in everything. Put all you are
> Into the smallest thing you do.
> The whole moon gleams in every pool,
> It rides so high.

The Drunken Tourist

The smallest thing to do was to stay as close to the heart of the moment as possible. Now, in the name of disaster, I *had* to concentrate on the Power of the Present. The alternatives were all fear. Looking back was killing me and the future was worse. Of course, at first, I would revert elsewhere every chance my mind could, but it hurt too much to stay there. Hard time is defined as wondering what is going down on the outside. The D.A. on my case was offering four years! And what about my boy, my love, my life! I refused to embrace any of it. I had to. I had to refuse to entertain any outside notions anymore. In the moment, I was cool. This was a good place. Now I could use the 'liberating power of affirmation.' "God, show me the way," was the first embrace. "God, show me the way," over and over. "Shut up and listen," is what I heard back. When I finally did shut up and listen, I was reintroduced to a naked little boy worth saving.

After seventeen days in that cell I got shipped to Wayside. Most everyone there was looking at real time and I was breaking down a lot. The conditions however, were much more humane. There was sky out the narrow windows looking out to the hills and there were a couple of cows on those hills. We got out once a week into the yard. Early on I got a pencil and some paper from Abraham – another drug casualty who was looking at too many years for a couple of dimes of crack. Guys like Abraham, with his incredible faith and indomitable sense of humor, got me grateful and kept me going. He would shout for "Prayer Call," just before count time every evening. These guys were praying for real. Arm in arm, the emotional energy of the prayers transcended all the crap. There was no recreational spirituality here. No Conversations with God, no Tao's of Pooh, no secret incantations that would conjure up God's deliverance, there was only sincere appeal. And everyone was praying mostly for their loved ones on the outside. Nobody claimed innocence.

In a week I was transferred to another dorm and was appointed to be a trustee for the serving line. We had our own cell of about thirty of us and the racial tensions going on were considerably less than in the general population. The equal number of blacks, whites and Hispanics might have helped. Also the perks were so numerous that nobody dared fuck around and get kicked back into the masses.

After about two weeks into the trustee thing, new melodies started to run through my head. I visualized the notes and attempted to write them down on hand drawn ledgers. Then I started to write a few short poems. Shortly after, songs started coming. I also struggled with a letter to Alex, even though I figured I wouldn't send it:

Hey Allie,
Dad still here. Did I ever mention that jail can be a real drag? Probably not. Probably because I can't afford to believe it. If I open that door, all the regret and guilt comes along with the territory. I am sorry to let you down. I hope you can forgive me. Of course I'm responsible for the harm that I have caused and have to pay for what I have done. This is going to take time. I hope you understand. I believe I can change for the better. Maybe you will notice – you know me better than anyone. I am not ashamed of myself anymore. This is where I had to go to get to where I am. It seems so long since we've been together, but I know when we see each other it will be like always. I feel so good with you around. I'm more proud of you than ever. Are you working on your tunes, your moves on the court and on the dance floor, your genuine rap and your general spread of good cheer? Someday you might try again to keep up with me. Around here the days move slow. I know it sounds strange, but one thing that is truly amazing is that everybody sort of loves one another. It's sort of like at school, when you might have gotten into a fight with your worst enemy, but once you're both in detention you're together. The scariest thing is not knowing what's going to happen. The way the courts go these days, two different guys with the same charge and the same record could get very different sentences. Injustice is everywhere; you just can't think about it. You just carry on Please, once again, learn from your Dad's mistakes. You know what a great example I am like that. ("Well son, will ya looka here, there's that road not to go down.") So many mistakes boil down to forcing what I want. Thinking I'm all that. Anyway, I did get 'love' recently. (Love is any kind of break you get from the powers that be.) I got 'hired' as a 'trustee.' We get to serve the food to the general population three times a day. There are forty of us line servers out of maybe 900 regulars in the cell block café. Nobody is ever late. We all have our jobs on

The Drunken Tourist

the line. We get the grub from the kitchen for the 'linebacker' to inspect as we wheel it to the dorms. The line boss' job is basically to get everybody nervous over nothing. Like he's going to get an early 'kick' (release) if we serve really well. We all get in a big hurry to serve food to everyone going nowhere. Much of jail is the old "hurry up and wait" deal. We wheel these long metal tables to the front of each dorm cell where the inmates wait in turn to get their tray. The meals are served when the deputy signals the 'linebacker,' who signals the 'breadman,' who is serving two to four slices of bread on to the tray depending on the meal. 'Trayman' does double duty by placing a packet of jelly or mayonnaise on the tray before sliding it about six inches to 'sporkman.' Sporkman is always in business no matter what we're serving. The tray goes down the line as fast as possible to 'vegman,' then 'meatman' (a coveted position), then to 'fruitman.' 'Cookieman' is usually the closest to the bars and he gets lots of shit from the clientele. Breakfast today was S.O.S. or Shit On a Shingle. This is a lumpy gravy meat medley poured over these thin little potato slabs about half an inch square. They look like little slabs of crack cocaine. Maybe this is good to remind many what got them here. The lumps in the gravy look like they might be burger meat but they're not. It smells too much like pork product, but it's not pork product either. Just eat it, alright already. Juiceman does either milk or sweet orange drink. Once in a while we get real juice in 4.5 ounce waxed cardboard containers. It is the general consensus that a smaller juice container can not be manufactured. The linebacker gets to call out the procedure as we move the metal tables from cell to cell. You bet we 'roll it out' then 'line it up,' to 'dish it out' before we 'roll em back' to 'scrape em off' then 'break it down.' Somebody always then says, 'It's Hammer time, break it down!' And we do a little jig. But you've got to watch 'radio' (noise level) or you'll get 'rolled up' and sent to the hole (you don't want to know). Alex, do you remember that joker MC Hammer? I'm going to tell your new girlfriend you used to love him. All in all, believe it or not, it may be easier to do a perfect day in here than on the outside. It's all a question of honesty. Honesty in the smallest of things.

Santana

That's how it goes anywhere, I suppose. In here, honesty creates integrity, and integrity is as big as you can get in here or anywhere else for that matter. I hope I can get mine. Yet another opportunity through disaster. Alex, remember you're the best. Believe it. Remember what you told me about your "life is life" theory. It's a good one.
I love you, Dad

* * *

Within the next week my family back east put together enough money to bail me out on the strict condition that I would have to go straight to a recovery house. My public defender thought the rehab would help me and help my case. His next line of defense was to stretch out my court dates long enough to show the court I was making some progress. Needless to say this was bigger than huge. I had a month to go before the preliminary hearing in Superior Court. Handcuffed and looking out gated windows, the bus ride at dawn from Wayside back to Central Jail was the most exciting ride of my life. Once back out on the street, in the shadow of Central Jail, I needed nothing. Not a dime, not a cigarette, not a marching band, not a thing. I was just taking my own sweet time through the beautiful slums of downtown Los Angeles. The views were magnificent, everyone looked dressed in their best, and the 1.5 Second road rule was now being observed or not.

The Luxurious Royal Palms

Business is brisk in the alley off Bonnie Brae and Sixth. Holiday balloons of heroin and doves of crack are moving in good quantity. From the window of Room 200, Robert, Rodney and I are witnessing all the action we were so recently such a part of. There's the main dealer we're calling King 3 Cart with his two lookouts down the way. Kids who have got a long way to go before they hit their bottoms, along with toothless, pregnant women are all getting theirs. And nobody is having any fun at all. Some of them put the dope in their mouths or cup it in their hand while doing that hurry up prequel to the Thorazene Shuffle out of the alley. Others are more casual, even kneeling behind a parked car to take a blast. A strawberry hooker that must have been cute even a couple of months ago squatted right below our window. Instead of lighting up, she pulled down her jeans and took a piss. Robert dashed to the bathroom, grabbed what was left of a roll of toilet paper and tossed it down to her, yelling "Merry Christmas." She looked up and sort of shrugged before she wiped and moved on. That used up wad of toilet paper might sit there well past New Year's.

* * *

So this is where you go when there's nowhere else to go. It's the last house on the block, in between the jailhouse and the mortuary. Considering the location, however, the place is downright plush. Guys are pushing shopping carts or even baby strollers up to the front stairs before checking in. Others are so stuck between a rock and a hard place that this place is just beautiful, thank you. I would be one of those guys. The first sign you see behind the front desk is "You are here to change, not to change things." What a pity, I thought. If given the chance, I could have done wonders redecorating.

I was soon to find redecorating was not an option here. Wholesale excavation was the only way to go. If I was lucky, I was going to be here for a while and the only way I was going to make it here was to do things their way. And the only way I was going to do things their way was to relax. The fight wasn't worth it. What was I going to do? Throw in my two cents and end up back in jail? I was tired as hell. Not only exhausted but tired of trying to make myself feel better. My way wasn't working and the extent that I didn't trust in anything besides myself was the extent that I wasn't happy. And I wasn't happy. My kingdom was sunk. This kingdom that was comprised of anything that looked good or felt good or smelled good. Whatever – if it came my way I was going to try to lay claim to it. I was sick of all that. So what was I in such danger of losing? My personality? Yeah right. My creative soul? Please. I wasn't throwing away the truth of my experiences – drinking or not, they were real. I was throwing away all those things I thought I knew about all those things I think. I was throwing away anything that made it harder to accept my situation. If not now, when?

In an attempt to get honest, I had told my son in his letter that there was opportunity through disaster. Well then, considering this obvious wreckage, this opportunity was huge. And if this place I had ended up in was such a dump, my dumpster was ready to unload.

In order to unload I had to follow instructions. Not that I necessarily wanted to. The whole idea of "program," had always made me sick… but not half as sick as the results of drinking and drugging made me. Trying to get away with anything now would result in a pain not worth the price of whatever petty victory I might achieve. Underneath the crude exterior and the bullshit attitudes, there were some people here that had been through a hell of a lot worse than me whom I had to trust. I had to trust somebody because I had to admit I needed help.

Mr. A taught me how to spell HUMILITY - something I didn't even have a 'nodding acquaintance' with. This was both a principal

The Drunken Tourist

and a personality to be taken seriously. Mr. B, on the other hand, taught the truth behind the cool. "The same thing it took to get your baby hooked is gonna be the same thing it takes to keep her," was typical of Mr. B. Through all the meetings, it wasn't exactly what they said that really mattered. What I was being taught was not necessarily what I was being taught. So what if I wasn't in a cave in the Himalayas working this out while sharing porridge silently with Swami Snatchabanana. Besides, when I wasn't in all of these mandatory meetings, I was sharing laughs with Mr. C, the best roommate I ever had. Stephen C. had pulled in about a month before I did, with a shopping cart in tow. Sadly, he had to leave his hot rod on the corner. Fresh from a bad run, he had spent the majority of the year in county jail for a number of petty charges, one of them being reckless driving. Reckless driving with the shopping cart. He got pulled over burning down Alvarado on his four-wheeler with a cartload of recyclables. Originally, the charges included drunk driving and speeding, but the judge threw those out and gave him the reckless driving. A year or two before that, Steven had done a stint at another California correctional facility making an exorbitant amount of money as the head chef. The house with the wife and kids were all gone now in exchange for the street life. I call him "Juice Man." If anybody could live on the streets in style, it would be Stevie C.

Mr. D made it crystal clear that my convoluted concepts of God were getting in the way of my experience of Him. These concepts were bound to crumble and bring me down with them. Then I would drink or freak or both. Hell, I could change my philosophy more often than my socks, so what was I holding on to so desperately? It was my need to be right, to get away with as much as possible, and for my agenda to be everyone's priority. These needs were really a security blanket for my lack of faith. Meanwhile, my conscience was working overtime – looking mostly at other people. This collective "other people" was how I had thought of the world for so long. What I was forced to reckon with was how this conscience was naturally supposed to work: it was supposed to apply to me. "Start applying what you might say to other people to yourself." That whisper from Paris was imperative now. Once again, I had to believe that what I was being taught was not necessarily what I was being taught – there was something going on here that I wasn't in control of. And this small surrender made all the difference. I was not in control. What a fucking relief. It all didn't have to be so ultimate.

Instead of looking at ultimates, I had to start looking at what was really happening. I needed to create space for that power of the present to reside in me – not just to visit. This space had to be cultivated another way besides my own, otherwise it would be overgrown in no time. I had to believe that even if I dumped the self-importance, I could still be valuable. I had to remember that I was trying to stay out of the results business. Every time I was tempted to see how I was doing, how I was doing stopped doing. So I had to trust that I would be taken care of. Otherwise it was back to the same old me. And this same old me smelled lousy. The Promises as outlined on pages 83 and 84 of the Big Book was the first passage that I could swallow in this respect:

> "If we are painstaking about this phase of our development, we will be amazed before we are half way through. We are going to know a new freedom and a new happiness. We will not regret the past nor wish to shut the door on it. We will comprehend the word serenity and we will know peace. No matter how far down the scale we have gone, we will see how our experience can benefit others. That feeling of uselessness and self pity will disappear. We will lose interest in selfish things and gain interest in our fellows. Self-seeking will slip away. Our whole attitude and outlook on life will change. Fear of people and economic insecurity will leave us. We will intuitively know how to handle situations which used to baffle us. We will suddenly realize that God is doing for us what we could not do for ourselves. Are these extravagant promises? We think not. They are being fulfilled among us – sometimes quickly, sometimes slowly. They will always materialize if we work for them."

There was no denying this. And at this point, these options seemed

The Drunken Tourist

a whole lot broader than a couple of cocktails. And then what? I suppose everyone has their own pet evils and at least one of mine was a real barker. Be it in the church or the pub, my world was not the world I wanted to live in anymore. This had put me in a position I think they refer to as "fucked." There had to be another way to go. This "way" had to be impersonal enough not to be self-centered and personal enough to call my own. After all, I still needed to belong to something I felt good about. So I had to look for the source of all feel good instead of what appeared to feel good. Fresh in my head was where those appearances had left me - Jail. Now I had a chance to step out into what I didn't know and could never own. This put me in a position I think they refer to as "faith." For the first time in my life I was choosing to pay the fare on that vehicle I had been hopping on and off of for years.

Believing that the fare of faith was worth more than my own overblown sense of entitlement proved to free up space in the old dumpster. Yet there was still the danger that I would simply fill it up with new thoughts and ideas, and no matter how new and improved they were, I'd just end up lugging around a new and improved dumpster. And with that admission the only honest thing left to do was to remain available.

Enter the gift of real power. The space that was now freed through faith was actually designed to hold something larger than the dumpster itself. Imagine that. I could hold something larger than myself and at the same time it was holding me. The vehicle of my understanding was now completely outclassed by a souped up garbage can running on unlimited power. The race was over. What a relief. The prevailing sense that my time was running out, that dark cloud that had followed me for years, effectively disappeared right then and there. Yet the proof had to be in the stretch. And it wasn't about whether I could dance or fuck or do both at the same time. This round, it was about playing with the band. And suddenly, there was too much to do.

During the holiday season the house hosted a dance in the ballroom. Throughout the night, the light burned deep, hard, and consecutive in so many of us who only a few days ago thought our lives were over. At first it was easier for me to dance without a drink in my hands, but then I didn't know what to do with the freedom. Confidence is so fleeting and everything creatively worthwhile is so close to ridiculous. Looking around, however, it was clear that everybody gets uncomfortable and eventually nobody cares unless you're not trying. We've all got our own moves to work on. Tonight it was all about sliding smooth up into the deepest part of the dance floor. Tomorrow, who knew? I could be sliding back into a jail cell. So I figured I'd best get with it while the getting was good. Could God's will be what was going down, right about now? Well, duh, brother, where you been? "Oh yeah," I remembered. "I've been here before, and now I'm not leaving, not without a fight anyhow."

During the evening our choir did a new rendition of the gospel standard, "We Are Soldiers" to the old "Superfly" groove. We brought the house down to the largest crowd I've ever played for. Go figure. At the end of the day, I found myself getting right-sized by choice rather than by guilt, for a change. Getting carried away was a trait of mine that I could now possibly put to good use as the situation demanded, not as how I demanded the situation. This wasn't about getting normal or getting comfortable or becoming "a responsible member of society." This was about attempting to find what Hesse described as "unification of personality." An experience I knew as cooperation with the Power of the Present. I just had to live with it for a while, instead of the usual, "OK, that's cool, I got it, now let's move on." I just had to get used to this little bit of peace I was feeling. No shame in that. I might even get addicted.

A quick review of The Magister Ludi explained this challenge more concisely. On page 351, Hesse states it clearly:

> "Awakening,' it seemed, was not so much concerned
> with truth and cognition, but with experiencing
> and proving oneself in the real world. When you
> had such an awakening you did not penetrate any
> closer to the core of things, to truth; you grasped,
> accomplished, or endured only the attitude of your
> own ego to the momentary situation. You did not
> find laws, but came to decisions; you did not thrust
> your way into the center of the world, but into the
> center of your own individuality. That, too, was
> why the experience of awakening was so difficult to
> convey, so curiously hard to formulate, so remote

The Drunken Tourist

from statement. Language did not seem designed
to make communications from this realm of life.
If, once in a great while, someone were able to
understand, that person was in a similar position,
was a fellow sufferer or undergoing a similar
awakening."

Perfectly powerful. So why was I so willing to listen to Herman Hesse
and not the suggestions of another alcoholic? I knew myself well
enough to figure there was no real danger in becoming the poster
boy in the parking lot of old-timers' catch phrases. And deep down I
could not deny the satisfaction of a good meeting. These folks were
playing for real. Getting through the hard stuff, sure, yet right along
with it, having a blast - mostly by making fun of themselves. This
was a reality I could deal with. Just being focused on something
other than myself must have a lot to do with it, too.

So was it strictly a question of ego? A question of pride? Easier to
relate to a dead author than someone going through much the same
as myself? Let's face it, I still wanted to be considered a special and
more compelling case than the next guy. Concentrating on someone
else was nice for a change, but c'mon now, I had to get back to my
own thing. My important stuff. Again with the bullshit.

To show up and allow things to happen was such a good deal that
it was the hardest thing in the world for me to do. Whether it was
at a meeting or at a piano – to achieve balance between what I
needed to say and what was best for the present had always been
the deal. This balance, if it was to be achieved in any conscious
degree, would have to become an acquired skill. And the only
way to acquire this skill was to stop trying to look like the finished
product before the product was finished. In the middle of the
Mediterranean or in the middle of rehab, the artisans of life that
were succeeding in this balance were consistently acting on other
people's needs. Creativity came through them in the sincere interest
of their fellows. "How can I help?" has to be the noblest of all call-
ings, while "I'm here to do whatever it takes," has to be the hardest
instrument to master. Meanwhile, these men and women offered a
glimpse into the proof of the matter – a reasonable degree of hap-
piness and satisfaction along the way.

Santana

At the end of all those obligatory meetings, this ideal was being stated repeatedly:

> "Our book is meant to be suggestive only. We realize
> we know only a little. God will constantly disclose
> more to you and to us. Ask Him in your morning
> meditation what you can do each day for the man
> who is still sick. The answers will come, if your own
> house is in order. But obviously you cannot transmit
> something you haven't got. See to it that your
> relationship with Him is right, and great events will
> come to pass for you and countless others. This is
> the Great Fact for us.
> Abandon yourself to God as you understand
> God. Admit your faults to Him and to your fellows.
> Clear away the wreckage of your past. Give freely of
> what you find and join us. We shall be with you in
> the Fellowship of the Spirit, and you will surely meet
> some of us as you trudge the Road of Happy Destiny.
> May God bless you and keep you – until then."

Good news for sure. I especially like the part, "we realize we know only a little." So what if I wasn't one of those that finally felt "home" when they hit the rooms of A.A. So what if the Big Book would never be scripture for me. Even scripture would never be scripture for me. And who trusts anyone that reads only one book anyhow? I'm the type that looks out for landmarks when traveling, and here was another Arc de Triomphe.

Maybe I'm lucky I got a little religion in me, but that's not gonna save me. I have to save me. I've gotta stick with the great gift that's been with me from the start – the great compass. I mean c'mon, how many gutters have I been in just to see the moon rise so high? Shakespeare got it right with, "to thine own self be true." I know when I'm pretending and hopefully I know when I'm "striking step with eternity." I'm not sure if I'll ever be able to completely surrender my will for God's will, but I could certainly put a greater purpose in front of my own. I've just gotta remember. Sure, I've got more than my share of making up to, but restraining myself has never been my strong suit. Getting out there and doing some good might be a better way to go. Yet as Reneé said back in Berlin, "there are some things I

The Drunken Tourist

don't need to know." Not yet, anyhow.

Tests lie ahead, and lie ahead they should, as we blaze our own trail on the common path. Whether this path was true could be determined by my compass and a sense of joy in my fellow travelers, no matter how things might appear.

And sure, sometimes I feel the need for validation – like on that little boat in Sausalito, when I was looking for that exclusive, limited engagement – looking for the halo. But really, what fun would that be? Turns out my truth has always been the same; I'm not looking for a limited engagement. It's my leap of faith – again and again and again. This leap isn't about drinking or not drinking, A.A. or my way, or any conversion to any "way." It's about what's right for the best. Right Now.

* * *

Before New Years, I reported to the Probation Department to interview for their recommendations to the Judge. My lawyer was confident that he could work out a deal with the D.A. after the preliminary hearing in Superior Court and before a trial date was set. After all, he said, they didn't have a case on the felony charge, and they knew it.

During the previous hearing, one of the arresting officers had testified that nobody knew that the cop who got hurt was even on the scene. And everybody had made such a federal case over the fact that I was so drunk. My worst liability was now my best defense.

The probation officer explained that it was his job to file a report as if I had already entered a plea. The Judge would review his report along with the rest of the paperwork regarding the case. The interview went better than I expected. I felt hopeful.

* * *

I went back to court on January 8th in my best suit, prepared to accept what was coming to me. After reading the probation report and conferring with the D.A., the Judge doubled my bail to $200,000 and threw me back in jail on the spot. My knees buckled.

Epilogue

The Songs
1. She's Such A Punk
2. Sailor's Song
3. Knuckleheads
4. Cash and Prizes
5. Precious Planet Dirt
6. Scared Little Kids
7. Messin' With Pete
8. Say Anything
9. The Truth vs. Everything Else

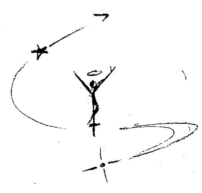

Black Market Trio is:
Tony Spicer, saxophone
Westin Young, drums
Chris Santana, vocals and piano

Track 3 was written by Tony K. - the exceptional painter from the Lower East Side who, when last seen, was working on gigantic canvases of snake-charmers. I hope he gets a hold of this and gets in touch.
The tunes can be heard at www.victorpress.org

Thanks,
Chris

12/10/10

To Michael
Thanks
Santana

She's Such A Punk

Jennifer A. Jackson has her mind and soul united
for the single purpose to, create spectacular,
whatever she wants to
It could be sugar, could be blood – she's such a punk we eat it up
Still looking for that brand new heavy – hey, hey, hey
She's such a punk but what a mother of a dream
Jennifer and Richard read, Virginia Woolf together
They said let's get this straight and split the rent forever
We'll have our cake and eat it too
we'll just find someone else to use
Still looking for that brand new heavy – hey, hey, hey
She's such a punk but what a mother of a dream
But Jenny and Dickie, all they did was party away the aggravation
Jenny said I'm sorry, but all this got to stop,
I see a lack of my own true nature
It could be cigs, it could be booze – and a ton of it won't do
Still looking for that brand new heavy – hey, hey, hey
She's such a punk but what a mother of a dream
So she hitched upon a star, left the earth behind,
caught a lucky breeze
Leaned a little bit harder, made it way past Mars,
another constellation please
See the planets shine, in all their brilliance – all right
Still looking for that brand new heavy – hey, hey, hey
She's such a punk but what a mother of a dream
But Jenny had her Granny's brains, so she got down on her knees
Said, "Lord, I don't really know you, But anyway it's me
So if you're half of what they say you are –
Can you spare a slice of that old pie?
Could you be my brand new heavy? hey, hey, hey
What a mother of a dream.

Sailor's Song

I've been a sailor on that sea of heartbreak
I am a sailor now that seeks no shore
Out here the wind and the waves take hold of fate
Out here you deal with what's dealt no more.
It's true... Almost too good... And it's all here for the asking
Ridin' them waves with the breeze,
can't come back till I made it
All the way around... go on... hang the doubt
I'm rolling all the way... Why worry now
I am enlisted in the good king's navy
I am enlisted as I choose to be
I set my course with the stars, they don't lie
I'll take the tour, I salute my charge
It's true... Almost too good... And it's all here for the asking
Ridin' them waves with the breeze,
can't come back till I made it
All the way around... go on... hang the doubt
I'm rolling all the way... Why worry now
I sing this sailor's song of sweet surrender
The storm's coming, the storm will pass
My oldest fear is now my favorite gal
The time is now...it's not mine
It's true...Almost too good...And it's all here for the asking
Ridin' them waves with the breeze,
can't come back till I made it
All the way around... go on... hang the doubt
I'm rolling all the way... Why worry now
Why worry now, why worry now?

Knuckleheads

(The Ballad of Juanita and Romeo)

The dog is barking in the yard
Juanita's kids are screaming mad
Music so damn loud, can't think, can't hear the beating
Daddy stumbles in the room
All eyes just stare in a pickled laugh
He says, "now get this straight
you little brats don't look at me like that"
Strike up the Band for the Undertaker
Ignorance fuels the mindless makers
Giving up on life
One flame flickers then it's back on top
Mobile homes, aluminum siding
Romeo's Scorpio's rising
Living it up he's a bad-ass boy
Beats his girlfriend up
It's a mad, mad, mad time
The friends all come around at eight
They say hey who's got the cards
Have a drink and talk about their empty lives
Juanita says, "there must be a better way"
She almost laughs out loud but hey,
She knows, she's angered him tonight
Strike up the Band for the Undertaker
Ignorance fuels the mindless makers
Giving up on life
One flame flickers then it's back on top
Mobile homes, aluminum siding
Romeo's Scorpio's rising
Living it up
He's a bad-ass boy
Beats his girlfriend up
It's a mad, mad, mad time

Cash and Prizes

We say we want it all
Home and family fame and fortune
Oh yeah and then there's God
I almost forgot, I should be grateful
I'm not that guy, the guy on the corner I just gave a dime to
Sure I could give more
But I've gotta save, I've gotta look out for my own
See the world will surely recommend
Choose your friends right, get ahead
And the world suggests now let's be real
First things first and that's the rent
I'm not mad as hell, let's just say I'm disappointed
You put your cards on the table
Play some gimme-gimme rummy
You put your cards on the table
And what do you got? What do ya got? What do we win?
Cash and Prizes
So I'm dreamin' up this noble plan
Make it big then give it back
But to only those that do deserve
A piece of mine, it makes me feel better
See the compromise is for the mediocre
The followers that don't dare better
As I catch myself at the mirror
There I am, another human being
See the world will surely recommend
Choose your friends right, get ahead
And the world suggests now let's be real
First things first and that's the rent
I'm not mad as hell, let's just say I'm disappointed

Precious Planet Dirt

Elise woke up lay still to wait
For the light of the day
This was time for her to share
Everything with her maker
She wouldn't dare to entertain
Thoughts no longer good for them
Or their Precious Planet Dirt
The blue would come right through the space
Between the shade and canopy
But today the sun was late
The birds confirm with their quickening
Up and out the door she blew
That reckoning had started
Just to see for sure the beauty of the day
Just to recognize, kinda right along with
How really big it's going to be
Her knees went out her head just bowed
Her face and hands they hit the mud
Wet and cold she didn't move
As her soul danced round the neighborhood
She buried deep right then and there
Thoughts no longer good for them
Or their Precious Planet Dirt
Just to see for sure the beauty of the day
Just to recognize, kinda right along with
How really big it's going to be
Just to see one lover, just to breathe one life
Coming clean she made a list of all folks to be closer with
What she might just do for them and their Precious Planet Dirt
Then all day long her people called, said it's time to right a wrong
Elise agreed

Scared Little Kids

Suzie's looking for work, we have much in common
Our dads have recently past, she lives in my old apartment
Dinner was planned, then she got busy fast
That all-important, noble cause
Rationale, is kickin' in and kickin' me out
I overheard you as you piss and moan
About your lack of love, your lack of that special one
Take away that thrill, we've got one scared little girl
Alice shops at the thrift, we have much in common
We go for the classics, hearts are warmed when we find bargains
How can I walk away, got to get to know you baby
That all-important, noble cause
Rationale, is kickin' in and kickin' me out
She'll take her treasures home, she'll bury them
Take care of them and share them with that special one, one day
Take away that thrill, take away them big big deals
We've got one scared little girl
But I do the same... I look at the face
I search for imperfections... That's where I concentrate
But the girl I met last night she took the cake all right
A radiation chocolate-covered birthday cake for Andrea
Our eyes met, right there we kissed,
It's bon voyage, she's off to Paris
That all-important, noble cause
Rationale, is kickin' in and kickin' me out
I don't believe it as I piss and moan about my lack of love
My lack of that special one
Take away that thrill, take away that old ridiculous
Take away my big fat ego, we got four scared little kids

Messin' With Pete

What we got here is a part of a soul that can never be shaken
Unforsakable, unforgettable… friend
Then again we got a head that is all about just looking good
What's been looking good might explode in your face
And it's been Messin' with Pete
His soul is going to meet up
His soul is going to meet with himself
Peace flows through the pain of change or rot
Teach me not to accept what will fade
First we pretend then protect what we think that we want is best
Then a love light rips through the pores of the flesh
It's been Messin' with Pete
His soul is going to meet up
His soul is going to meet with himself
Knock down Peter
His soul is gonna meet up
His soul is gonna meet with himself
Harvest comes
I'll throw away the rotten ones
I'll keep the good I've waited for… so long
My beloved is calling me
My beloved is calling me
Never, never to be forgotten

Say Anything

Hey buddy, why you so cold?
Hey buddy, why you so cold?
Is that the way you want it to be?
Is that the way you were brought up to be?
Thinking everyone wants a little piece of that shine
Nod or Something
Say anything
Who cares who's listening
It's probably just the usual
I can't believe it walking down the street
Eyes are on the down they're on the newsprint
Whatever happened to – hey, how ya doin'?
I can't believe someone would actually say to me
So much for that other guy now he's a deadbeat
Whatever happened to lookin' out for someone else
Nod or Something
Say anything
Who cares who's listening
It's probably just the usual
You can keep on walking and say your little prayers
And if you believe in spirit beings they might be listening too
There goes another heart, hard as rock, outside in the cold
Find a way, no don't shy away, find a way, no don't shy away
One step for a cause, for a cause to discover
Nod or Something
Say anything
Who cares who's listening
It's probably just the usual
You can keep on walking and say your little prayers
And if you believe in spirit beings they might be listening too

The Truth Vs. Everything Else

When I was nine, they kept saying
Just keep believing, just keep believing
When you're dead, dead and buried
You'll know the reason, you'll know the reasons
But in this world, we live, it feels good, to get rid of it
Here's to the Death of Magical Thinking
Here's to the fall of nothing real
I suppose, but I don't really know
It's Truth vs. Everything Else
Now who's the brain that told me
You've got these three little words
And who's the brains that told me here
You gotta put in your forty years
Well I'm halfway there and I know a little bit less
I'll take the drunken drowning man any day
Here's to the Death of Magical Thinking
Here's to the fall of nothing real
I suppose, but I don't really know
It's Truth vs. Everything Else
Light the fires, fan the flames
It's going down page by page
I made my mind up
No I'll change it again
I got a chance here to stop pretending
Here's to the Death of Magical Thinking
Here's to the fall of nothing real
I suppose, but I don't really know
It's Truth vs. Everything Else